More than 60 t
the devastation of abortion

EMPTY
ARMS

Wendy Williams and Ann Caldwell

"In 1993, Chattanooga, Tennessee became the first mid-sized city in America to close the doors of its neighborhood abortion clinic. Three years later the National Memorial for the Unborn was begun to offer peace to post-abortive parents, to remember babies who have been lost to abortion and to offer the hope of salvation. This book tells life-giving stories of forgiveness and hope that some have found through Christ."

Christian Medical and Dental Association

"Women think that abortions will fix things, but this book exposes this thinking as a lie. Each woman's story reveals the horror of the procedure, long-term physical consequences, and emotional despair resulting from her abortion. These heart-wrenching stories are graphic and painful to read, but each woman has found hope and forgiveness in Christ. Healing has also come by naming the baby, placing the name on a plaque, and adding it to The Memorial Wall of Names at The Memorial to the Unborn in Chattanooga, Tenn.
"This book should be required reading for every teenage girl... Excellent for the church library but possibly with a note warning of graphic subject matter."

JST, Church Libaries, Evangelical Church Library Association

Empty Arms: Remembering the Unborn
© 2005 by Wendy Williams and Ann Caldwell

All rights reserved. Except for brief quotations in printed reviews, no part of this publication may be reproduced, stored in a retrieval system or transmitted in any form or by any means (printed, written, photocopied, visual electronic, audio, or otherwise) without the prior permission of the publisher.

Unless otherwise indicated, all Scripture quotations are taken from the HOLY BIBLE, NEW INTERNATIONAL VERSION®. NIV®. Copyright ©1973, 1978, 1984 by International Bible Society. Used by permission of Zondervan Publishing House. All rights reserved.

ISBN 978-1-7332344-3-6

First edition—January 2005

Second edition–January 2020

Cover designed by Noah Craig, Chattanooga, Tennessee
Interior design and typesetting by Reider Publishing Services, West Hollywood, California
Edited and Proofread by Agnes Lawless, Dan Penwell, Sharon Clark Goodrich, and Warren Baker

Printed in the United States of America

I dedicate this to my wonderful husband Mark who held me during endless nights of weeping over my lost baby. He has been a driving force behind this project and speaks boldly for the rights of the unborn. I thank the Lord for our children, Mac, Kay, and Ben, who bring us such joy.

—ANN CALDWELL

I dedicate this to Henry, my life partner of thirty years, who has encouraged me throughout the process. His willingness to console a newborn and change diapers reflects a gentle Christ-like kindness.

I want to thank each of our children: Evan, Kira, Tacy, and Eric, who have loved, supported, and prayed for the tiny infants God has placed in our care over the years.

—WENDY WILLIAMS

And we both dedicate this to our heavenly Father.

The eternal God is your refuge,
and underneath are the everlasting arms.
Deuteronomy 33:27

The contents of this book include some graphic descriptions of problems relating to crisis pregnancies. Parents may wish to use caution in sharing with children.

We hope that you will contact us if you are inspired to place a plaque at the Memorial. God may allow us to publish another volume of stories from the Wall, in the future, and we welcome your submission.

In 2018 the National Memorial for the Unborn provided:

- 158 brass name plates on the wall, memorializing children lost through abortion

- 17 brick pavers in the garden, memorializing children lost through miscarriage

- 106 Certificates of Life, naming and honoring the identities and lives of children lost through preborn death

Contact us at: memorialfortheunborn.org
6230 Vance Rd.
Chattanooga, TN 37421
(423) 899-1677
Our financial support comes primarily from individual and corporate donors as well as church partnership. We welcome contributions.

Contents

Foreword
ix

Acknowledgments
xv

Introduction
xvii

History of the National
Memorial for the Unborn:
End the Massacre
1

Experiencing The Memorial
9

Whispers from The Wall:
Stories of the Unborn
17

EMPTY ARMS

POEMS FROM THE WALL
178

CRIES FROM THE CRADLE:
STORIES OF ADOPTION
194

EPILOGUE
222

INDEX AND LOCATION OF
PLAQUES AT THE WALL
224

FOREWORD

OVER THE LAST several years, the National Memorial for the Unborn has become a special place for remembering. Women and family members who have experienced abortions have come to The Memorial to shed tears, to remember, and to honor their unborn babies. Many of those who've come have left their stories. It's exciting now to witness the process of placing these stories into a collection, thanks to the efforts of Memorial board members, Ann Caldwell and Wendy Williams.

Most accounts in this book come from those whose arms are empty because of abortion. They are eulogies remembering the children they may have held but who are now held in heaven. The stories also represent experiences of men and women who have been made whole through confession. They are expressions of remorse and then of healing. But even before this, they reveal the great difficulty women have in facing unplanned pregnancies.

In my medical practice I had a patient who found herself newly pregnant. With a surprised and fearful look in her eyes, she wondered what to do. Being pregnant was her immediate, overwhelming concern, but holding a baby, for some reason, seemed a more distant concept.

Why was this the case? My patient was facing a major dilemma. As we talked, I began wondering what was happening in our culture that was separating pregnancy from having and holding babies? We live in a society of multiple options with emphasis on the mother's choice. One option is the right of abortion. Physicians today, as a matter of ethics, are trained to respect personal autonomy in making decisions. Gone are the days when I could simply tell a pregnant mother what she should do in regards to an unplanned pregnancy. Or are those days gone?

Must a physician remain passive when a young, pregnant woman decides to abort for whatever reasons are deemed necessary? Should we as a society remain neutral, even silent, so freedom of choice may proceed unabated?

In most medical encounters, it is considered best to give full disclosure, informing the patient as completely as possible about the positive and negative effects of any medical plan. This is called informed consent, and is considered ethically important. Yet too often since the *Roe v. Wade* decision, one hears a doctor's advice that sounds something like this: *You can get this over in ten minutes, and then you can forget completely about it.*

Many abortions occur for lack of information from a medical provider. Sometimes there is no medical visit. In other cases the guidance is minimal. Yet it has been shown that when women are given details about babies forming in the uterus, abortions occur less often. This is human life, after all, not just a "blob of tissue." If pregnancy continues just four or five weeks, an ultrasound test can show evidence of a beating heart. In one report from a crisis pregnancy center in Ohio—with no ultrasound administered—just 20% of abortion-minded clients continued with their pregnancies. But when an ultrasound was administered, 95% of the women continued on with their pregnancies. When a woman is confronted with proof of life, her choice is likely to change dramatically.

Physicians have an obligation to inform their patients of the possible outcomes of choices they make. Women should know that new lives are involved. They should know the consequences of abortion—infertility, the risk of other medical problems, the post-abortion emotional effects. They should also know the positive options available for dealing with unplanned pregnancies.

Patients, too, have ethical responsibilities. Yet there is a difficulty here, for the legacy of our culture involves a giant cover-up in the name of choice. Women are told to choose whatever they like, to forget, and to move on. In reality, this is asking for trouble.

A frightening consequence of abortion is that a large number of abortions are repeats. Many women have said that when they got pregnant, they aborted again in order to punish themselves for the first abortion—as if they could somehow atone for their initial mistakes. As they manipulate their own consciences, they hurl themselves into further wrong.

The mothers, fathers, and grandparents whose stories and eulogies are written in this book know that honest confession concerning past experiences is best. Many also look to their abortions as markers of positive changes in their lives, yielding opportunities for healing. A great number of these women and men are becoming whole again through repentance and faith in the Author of life. Many of them come to the National Memorial for the Unborn, which stands not only in memory of millions of babies that have died, but also to remind future generations that God is faithful to forgive and to keep His promises.

The book also includes stories that express different experiences—the emptiness of arms that have rescued babies and then let them go to others. These accounts are from families that have cared for infants that might have been aborted but whose birthmothers decided on an adoption plan. The empty arms of these stories have held babies for a time in the work of saving them from death and then releasing them for a lifetime. These are the arms of foster or interim-care parents who stand in the gap between birth and adoption.

My wife, Wendy, and I have cared for dozens of babies awaiting adoptive placement over the years. We have held babies as newborns, sometimes for weeks of interrupted nights, until the placement plans were completed. Our own children have held, fed, and watched them grow. Emotions run strong, yet we have joined in this rescue process to help encourage positive solutions to crisis pregnancies.

Many have asked how we can let these babies go after the natural attachment that occurs in caring for them. They wonder if such work takes too great a toll on us. We can only tell of the great joy that comes in helping to save and nurture new lives, and assisting young women who decide to allow this. We also hurt deeply for those who have had abortions, who could have found alternatives if someone had reached out to them.

As we have emptied our arms at adoptive placements in

which we have participated, our lives have become richer. We take heart as we see that life has been chosen for a new little one, both by the birthmother and by the adoptive family. Yet we also think of those who have followed different paths in crisis pregnancies. We are thankful that many of these individuals are finding restoration and healing. Their stories are here, and this book is for them. It is also for readers who may have found themselves in similar situations. May they find comfort and restoration as well, and may they know the God of all comfort "because the one who is in you is greater than the one who is in the world" (1 John 4:4).

—Henry Williams, M.D., F.A.C.P.

Acknowledgments

 HIS BOOK would not have been possible without the courageous men and women who gave permission to share their stories. And so we thank God for their courage and healing.

"He who sacrifices thank offerings honors me,
and he prepares the way so that I may
show him the salvation of God."
Psalm 50:23

We also appreciate the kind assistance and prayers of the following people:

Linda Keener Thomas, who began this project in 1997
The staff at Bethany Christian Services
Dr. Dennis Bizzoco
Rev. Robert Borger
Vicki Butters

Mark Caldwell
Covenant Trucking
Richard Crotteau
Ray Harvey
Michael Jennings
Mareta Keener
Pat Lindley
Grete Lombardy
Terry McCaulley
All members of the Pro-Life Coalition
Sally Morrison
Rita Sigler
Henry Williams
Tacy Williams Beck

We gratefully acknowledge Dan Penwell and the staff at AMG Publishers who were brave enough to take on this project.

And Dave Worland, Noah Craig, and Rick Steele.

And fellow Board members for the National Memorial for the Unborn:

Rob Allen	Carol Martin
Lance Irwin	Kristin Smith
Wanda King	Debra Choate
Jim Steed	Amy Scott
Anne Swafford	Kelli Combs

May God be blessed because you love Him.

INTRODUCTION

by Ann Caldwell

EVERY DAY thousands of babies are killed and lives are altered permanently by the lie of abortion. That's what *Empty Arms* is about—relationships broken, goals and ambitions destroyed, hurt upon hurt heaped on loved ones, denial, drugs, rape, and tears—*lives changed forever.* Dear reader, please realize that for every story you see here, thousands upon thousands are untold because of the shame, guilt, and fear associated with abortion.

This book is also about *hope,* because each individual has found salvation through Christ. These stories have been collected to honor the babies, to honor the Lord Jesus, and to show you the widespread impact of abortion on families. The people who have contributed their testimonies are on the other side of very painful experiences, and we're grateful that they are willing to share so openly.

For the reader who may be considering an abortion, you have been and remain in our prayers. We want you to read these stories before you take action, to imagine your life after an abortion. We hope these stories will give you a sense of the enormous impact abortion has on people's lives. As you read, please keep in mind that most of these situations occurred prior to ultrasound technology. At that time, many women believed the lie that "it's just tissue" because there was no concrete evidence that it was a baby. Now we have conclusive evidence. We encourage you to go to your local crisis pregnancy center for education, an ultrasound (if it's available), and good counsel. If you have been through an abortion, please refer to our resource section at the end of this book and make contact with one of the many healing ministries listed.

Not long ago, I would have scoffed at the idea of a book entitled *Empty Arms* because I had had an abortion. I exercised my right to choose, which allowed me to continue my education at a prominent university. As a result of my horrible decision, I discovered the forgiveness that comes only through Jesus Christ.

One purpose of this book is to show that all women who have had abortions suffer afterwards. *Abortions do not solve problem pregnancies.* Amazingly, one out of four women has had an abortion, while countless families are trying to adopt children. There is a way out of this mess—and it must not be kept a secret.

History of the National Memorial for the Unborn
End the Massacre

Jeannie St. John Taylor

THE CHATTANOOGA Women's Clinic Inc. loomed across the street and catty-corner to the strip mall where the tiny AAA Women's Services, a crisis pregnancy center, kept an office. Unregulated and unkempt and yet lucrative, the Chattanooga Women's Clinic had stood unchallenged since 1975. No one monitored the health and safety of the girls who exited its doors empty and bleeding.

The sight of this abomination dominating a city known for its churches sickened many Christians. Nevertheless, an eerie helplessness hung over the people like smog. They endured Chattanooga's disgrace in silence... until 1989, when the Pro-Life Coalition of Chattanooga took a public stand.

In recognition of the sixteenth anniversary of the *Roe v. Wade* decision, the Coalition organized a public funeral procession to grieve the thousands of babies murdered at the clinic. They feared that only the handful that helped set up the rally would turn out on the appointed day. Instead, borrowed hearses led three hundred packed cars and a thousand people along the nine-mile route to the clinic. On the street in front of the clinic, college students held up a banner declaring the procession "In Memory of the Babies Who Died in This Place." Local florists donated flowers to lay on the line that had been painted to prevent concerned citizens from approaching the building.

The fight was engaged. In homes all over the city, believers began to pray.

A few months into the battle, at six o'clock on a Sunday morning, a handful of grieving men and women from diverse denominations—Catholic, Presbyterian, evangelical, charismatic—formed a circle in the parking lot of the abortion clinic. Joining hands and voices, they lifted cries to God, begging him to end abortion in Chattanooga. *Lord, change the hearts of the owners and operators of the clinic, or remove them from the scene*, they prayed.

Sunday after Sunday the community of believers gathered in the parking lot to pray. And behind the scenes, the King of heaven wove events on earth.

NATIONAL MEMORIAL FOR THE UNBORN

Within six months, the fifty-three-year-old owner of the abortion business was diagnosed with pancreatic cancer. She died six months later. Her financial partner took over the operation of the clinic. Shortly afterward, doctors diagnosed the partner, at age fifty-one, with another type of cancer. She, too, died within months.

Still, the abortions continued. Earlier, the two women had signed a five-year lease with the wealthy Realtor who owned the building. This lease allowed the abortionist to continue slaughtering babies for profit.

Sunday morning parking-lot prayers intensified.

On a Thursday evening in April 1993, the Pro-Life Coalition held its quarterly meeting. Patricia Lindley, the Coalition president, had received word of a remarkable turn of events.

At the meeting, Dr. Dennis Bizzoco informed the other board members, "A doctor friend called to tell me that the owner of the clinic building is in bankruptcy. He has to sell the building, and guess who's buying it?"

Without hesitation, someone answered, "The abortionist."

"My friend learned about it because the owner of the clinic owes him $128.00," said Dr. Bizzoco. "That gives him standing in bankruptcy court. And because of that, he can take a bid in for us."

"It's true," responded attorney Richard Crotteau. "They may have wanted to keep it a secret, but a Christian Realtor I know confirmed the information. It's pretty much a done deal right now. The abortionist already bid $254,000. All that's left is the paperwork. The sale will be final at 5 p.m. Monday. And we have somewhere around $1,600 in our treasury. That wouldn't even buy the sidewalk."

"Even if we could come up with the money, they'd just find another facility," someone said.

Dr. Bizzoco's next statement put the discussion in a new context. "If the Lord is giving us the opportunity to engage the enemy in battle, we dare not shrink back."

"Then the question for us becomes clear," said Pastor Bob Borger. "If we ask Him for the funds and that amount of money becomes available, we'll know that this is what the Lord wants us to do."

Murmurs of agreement spread through the group. They joined hands in prayer around the conference table. After prayer, all individuals in the group felt they should call as many people as possible, asking for donations. They left that night needing to raise over a quarter of a million dollars by Monday—slightly more than seventy-two hours away! Everyone knew that only the Lord could accomplish such an impossible task.

God spoke to Chattanooga's community of believers, and they responded. Money poured in. One young couple contributed a check for over seven thousand dollars—money they had saved for a new car. An elderly woman unfolded a lace handkerchief filled with crumpled bills and a few coins, giving the Coalition everything she had—fourteen dollars and twenty-three cents.

Large and small, the funds came in. By noon on Monday, the Coalition had $241,000 toward the purchase. Attorneys Michael Jennings and Richard Crotteau prepared the legal documents offering $254,000 for the structure. They arrived at the Federal Courthouse just fifteen minutes before the sale of the building to the abortionist would have been final. The sale was halted; a higher bid had come in. The proceedings would now be handled in a bidding war in the courtroom. On Friday morning, members of the Pro-Life Coalition arrived in court with their attorneys. The abortionist's lawyers shuffled through papers on the other side of the courtroom. Tension sizzled in the air. The judge announced that the building would be auctioned off. Court would recess temporarily, then meet again at 1 p.m. to give the abortionist time to show up in person. On the way out of the courthouse, attorneys who had been in the courtroom listening to the proceedings contributed money to the Coalition. It was clear that what was at stake was far more than just a piece of property. Patricia felt as though they were living a Peretti novel where the presence of good and evil is so clearly defined. The prayer rising from the city to God's throne room was opening the way for God to work. All they could do was watch.

Money continued to flood in to the attorney's office. By one o'clock, members of the Coalition and their attorneys carried $301,000 in pledges, cash, and bank deposit slips into the courtroom. The abortionist glowered at them from across the aisle. The bids would be in five-thousand-dollar increments. He would bid against them in person.

"My clients will deal in cash," the Coalition's attorney informed the judge. She tapped a thick stack of money and deposit slips in her palm.

The abortionist started the bidding. "$269,000."

Staring straight ahead, the Coalition attorney countered with, "$274,000."

"$279,000." The abortionist spoke deliberately, glaring at them through narrowed, malevolent eyes.

"$284,000," said the Coalition attorney.

"$289,000." The abortionist spit out the words.

"$294,000." The Coalition attorney spoke confidently, forcefully, but those with the Coalition knew it was the Coalition's last bid. They had determined not to go beyond what the Lord had provided.

Silence.

The attorney shifted from one foot to the other. The judge looked at the abortionist expectantly. "To h—- with it!" muttered the abortionist.

Nothing could be heard but the sound of breathing.

The judge banged his gavel. Bam! "Sold to the Pro-Life Coalition!"

Outside the courtroom, cameras flashed as reporters thrust microphones toward Patricia Lindley. "Wasn't that a waste of the Coalition's money?" asked one reporter. "Did you know that the appraised value of the building was only $189,000?"

"You can never put a price tag on the value of even one human life," Patricia responded.

"Where did you come up with cash to buy the clinic?" another reporter asked.

"We had absolutely unlimited resources, because everything belongs to the God of heaven and earth," Patricia answered. "We prayed and the Lord answered."

Two weeks later, on May 15, the abortionist's lease ran out, and he performed his last abortion. On May 17, 1993, the Coalition closed the clinic. After gutting and remodeling it, they reopened the building—half of it as the new home of AAA Women's Services. For many years, "Sanctity of Human Life Sunday" was observed with a prayer vigil outside the building. On that Sunday in 1994, Christians joined in prayer as they dedicated the building to the Lord for His glory!

NATIONAL MEMORIAL FOR THE UNBORN

Because they viewed the clinic as holy ground, much as a Civil War battlefield is holy because of the lives lost there, they transformed the other side of the building into the National Memorial for the Unborn. More than 35,000 unborn babies had died in that place. It now stands as a testimony to the value of human life. It is a place where women and men from all over the nation can honor the children lost to abortion and seek the Lord's forgiveness.

Against all human logic, the abortionist never opened another facility. To this day, there is no abortion clinic in Chattanooga, Tennessee.

—Reprinted with permission from *101 Stories of Answered Prayer* by Jeannie St. John Taylor and Petey Prater.

*Rescue those being led away to death;
hold back those staggering toward slaughter.*
Proverbs 24:11

Experiencing The Memorial

 S YOU ENTER the wrought iron gates of The Memorial to the Unborn, directly in front of you in the courtyard is a white marble sculpture. The title is *In the Arms of an Angel,* created by Terry McCaulley, an artist whose home studio is in Taos, New Mexico.

On the other side of the courtyard are glass doors to a building that protects The Memorial Wall. The Memorial itself features a fifty-foot granite "Wall of Names" which holds thousands of small brass plates with words of remembrance placed by mothers, fathers, and other family members from all over the country. The Memorial is open twenty-four hours a day. Visitors from all over the world are visibly moved by the touching displays of affection in the form of stuffed toys, flowers, and notes left by family members. It inspires a time of reflection as a large, wooden cross towers in front of The Wall.

To the right of The Wall, you will see a large, stunning painting encased in glass. The title is *I'll Hold You in Heaven*, created by Ray Harvey from St. Louis, Missouri. Mr. Harvey was inspired to create this 4 x 6 foot painting of a woman embracing her infant close to her heart after he heard the amazing story of God's redemption and healing when Christians purchased the abortion clinic and made it into The Memorial.

When you leave The Wall there is a Remembrance Garden to the right and down a few steps. The Pool of Tears is dedicated to the memory of children lost to miscarriages. These babies are remembered through bricks placed in the garden with their names on them.

The stories in this book are only a sampling of the hundreds of letters the National Memorial for the Unborn receives every year, along with orders for plaques. The two stories below were contributed by the artists who were led by the Lord to donate their artwork to the National Memorial for the Unborn.

EXPERIENCING THE MEMORIAL

An Artist's Story
by Ray Harvey

In 1994 I heard a radio broadcast describing the story and vision for the National Memorial for the Unborn. After listening to a description of The Wall of Names, I knew I wanted to talk to these folks and perhaps create a piece of art they could use in their ministry. Since I was numb and ignorant to the reality of abortion, I had no idea what lessons were in store for me.

My completed painting made a big impact as it was displayed at locations and functions around the country. It traveled to the Focus on the Family headquarters in Colorado Springs and then to the National Right to Life Convention. Many churches and organizations invited me to speak about The Memorial and exhibit my piece.

I met a man one evening who caught me by surprise. After giving a talk to a small church one Sunday evening I was at the rear of the building to meet with people as they left. I saw him coming toward me. He looked tough. A biker I assumed, leather vest covered with patches, tattoos along his arms, and a bandanna on his head controlling the long hair that was stuffed underneath. This didn't look like it was going to be pretty. He quickly approached me and shoved his hand into mine.

"Thank you, Brother," he said. "I really enjoyed what you said. I only wish my wife could have been here. You see we have an abortion in our life. It's not a problem though. It was our decision and we regret it but it's O.K. It's not a problem. I wish she could have been here."

He continued rambling and I didn't know how to respond.

"Yeah, I really liked what you said. I wish she could have been here." He stopped for just an instant and looked me in the eye. I saw the remorse and I saw the lie.

He started to cry. "Well that isn't really the truth," he began. "You see, it is a problem. It's killing us. We can't even talk about it. It's tearing us apart. I wish she would have been here."

One moment this intimidating tough guy, the next a broken ashamed child. The look of *How did this happen?* was all over his face as I held the sobbing man in my arms. I saw how powerful the regret of abortion is and how it affects not just the women but also the men.

Again and again, I saw the powerful regret of abortion and how it affects men and women. I've often wondered how this panel of paint could have such effect on people. *I'll Hold You in Heaven* hangs permanently next to The Wall. I tell people that on the canvas there is a color that I do not know how to mix. It is the color of the Holy Spirit, and I have seen its reflection on those who view the painting. This original piece communicates the hope and forgiveness offered through Jesus on a site where once over 35,000 babies were aborted.

No other painting I have done has the strength and power of this image. We have already seen God do a great work of healing in many people's lives through it.

EXPERIENCING THE MEMORIAL

A Sculptor's Story
by Terry McCaulley

Terry shared his story when he visited The Memorial:

I was involved in a relationship where I tried to save my child but the mother chose abortion. It caused me much grief. Later, I was in another relationship when I had a powerful dream wherein I saw my unborn child in a beautiful garden filled with the Holy Spirit. Yet I experienced sorrow and grief. One month later I realized the dream was a warning of the events that were about to unfold.

Once again, the woman I was with found out she was pregnant and chose to abort the baby. I lovingly tried to change her mind, but again I was unsuccessful and the mother's choice was the only one heard. Each time my heart was torn in pieces. My faith in God and my renewed relationship with Jesus Christ helped me to experience His forgiveness for my choices, which were not in His good order and that had contributed to the women's decisions. Jesus gave me strength to walk through the turmoil of intense anger and grief. I was able to forgive each woman for her choice to abort.

The sculpture was started when I created an angel out of a piece of white marble. I remembered my mother told me she had a dream of an angel of mercy coming to help her make the journey into God's kingdom. One week later she passed on, so I wanted this to be made in honor of her memory.

I believe I am a co-creator with God. I asked Him to turn my grief, anger, and painful loss of my two children into love. He clearly answered my prayer when I added to the sculpture an unborn child resting in the arms of the angel. It was placed in a friend's gallery. As visitors saw the artwork it began to minister to them, encouraging them toward hope, love, and forgiveness. Sharing my story about the angel also helped me deal with my own deep pain.

Many expressed interest in buying the angel but I did not sell it. Later, I met Yvonne and Warren Williams who were amazed at the piece and told me about the existence of the National Memorial for the Unborn (NMU). I knew it was destined for this purpose. The sculpture would be a window into heaven on the site of the abortion clinic where so many babies were killed. Warren Williams began the purchasing process with a down payment. I then contacted the NMU to donate it to The Memorial, but the board members wondered how it would be transported.

God provided Covenant Trucking to move this beautiful piece from New Mexico to Tennessee, free of charge. On January 22, 2003, Sanctity of Life Sunday, the sculpture was permanently placed in front of the glass doors at the Memorial. I shared my thoughts with the crowd:

> *My hope is that others will be touched by the sculpture.*
> *I will be pleased to have this touch even one life so a child*
> *might be saved. I also want mothers and fathers to find*
> *healing in the peace of God, because He is so merciful.*
> *I want to encourage the men to be loving and supportive*
> *to the women in their lives. Both of you nurture your*

EXPERIENCING THE MEMORIAL

children with love and acceptance. My prayer is that everyone will come to believe that God created life and He alone should decide when life should return to heaven.

—Terry is now living near Taos, New Mexico, and is the proud father of two daughters.

God has surely listened and heard my voice in prayer. Praise be to God, who has not rejected my prayer or withheld his love from me!
Psalm 66:19, 20

Let the peace of Christ rule in your hearts . . . and be thankful.
Colossians 3:15

> Please honor us with your presence and experience The Wall for yourself. We are open 24 hours a day and we always welcome visitors.

Whispers from The Wall
Stories of the Unborn

ALIDA CHERISE HARLESS
March 14, 1995
Amazing Grace . . . How Very Sweet

I was sixteen when my father raped me. It had happened before. I didn't think anything would come of it, except more pain, self-hate, and hiding. Twelve weeks later, bleeding and searing pains began. My school nurse referred me to a local women's health center where I was pressured into having an abortion. Afterwards, I was completely numb as I pulled on my clothes and prepared to leave the clinic. I was sure of two things—I felt like God hated me for taking the life of my baby, and I would never tell anyone what had happened to me in that tiny room.

I soon pushed down all the feelings and emotions concerning the abortion and continued on with my life. I worked too many hours a week to make the grades that would keep me in the National Honor Society. I continued to amaze people with how well I managed, while inside, I felt as if I were dying.

Six months later, I could no longer ignore my feelings about my past. I decided to call a local church for some help. Instead, I dialed the wrong number—the Alternatives Pregnancy Center 24-hour hotline. I talked to a woman on the phone and went in a few days later where I found a safe place to share my pain. After some individual counseling, I joined a post-abortion Bible study. For the first time, I began to see light at the end of the tunnel. We ended the group with a wonderful memorial service for our lost babies. I began to feel a sense of closure, but my heart knew something was missing.

Just before another anniversary of my abortion came, I contacted the National Memorial for the Unborn. Through placing a plaque on The Wall and acknowledging the loss, I've been able to further grieve and process my feelings. I now feel an even bigger sense of closure and am building a stronger relationship with God. I thank Him for the Alternatives Pregnancy Center and the National Memorial for the Unborn, but most of all I thank Him for the support they've given me.

—Carrie Harless

*You are all sons of God
through faith in Christ Jesus.*
Galatians 3:26

> **ALLISON MARIE SHANNON**
> August 23, 1975
> *I Do Love You Now. Mom*

> **PATRICK MARK SHANNON**
> March 8, 1980
> *I Do Love You Now. Mom*

I was not raised in a Christian home. My mom died when I was eleven years old, and my dad was an alcoholic. When I was fourteen, an eighteen-year-old took advantage of me, and I became pregnant. A friend, who already had a couple of abortions, told me where to go and what to do. So I had my first abortion when my dad was on his honeymoon with my stepmother. She not only became his wife but also helped him to be sober, and he has been sober ever since.

I became very rebellious after that abortion and I began to use drugs, alcohol, and people. Five years later, I became pregnant again. Because abortion is legal in the United States, I knew where to go and what to do—I had my second abortion at the age of nineteen.

And now the good news: four months after that second abortion, I gave my heart to Jesus and became a new creation. I knew and felt His cleansing at that moment of salvation. Three years later, I married my pastor. I became depressed after four years without conception. Because of my low self-esteem due to my post-abortive condition, I was critical of others to make myself look good.

As a married woman desiring children, I had begged God to give me a child. Although I did not know it at the time of my abortions, I came to realize that I had killed my two children. And now I wanted a child desperately. I had exploratory surgery and did conceive. Ten months later, Seth was born! When Seth was two years old, I attended a post-abortion Bible study at a crisis pregnancy center. God used His Word to bring healing. Although my sins had been forgiven at my salvation, I had never forgiven myself and the others involved with my abortions. Nearly four years after Seth's birth, Ruth arrived.

Two years later, I went to Chattanooga with friends and placed my first two children's names on The Wall at the National Memorial for the Unborn, which completed my healing. Since Jesus bore my shame on the cross of Calvary, I am no longer ashamed. Since then I've had another son, John. I'm the proud mother of five—Seth, Ruth, and John are here with me, and Allison and Patrick are waiting for me in heaven with Jesus. What a truly blessed woman of God I am! "To God be the glory—great things He has done."

—Crystal Shannon Henderson

*Therefore, if anyone is in Christ,
he is a new creation; the old has gone,
the new has come!*
2 Corinthians 5:17

*To all who received him,
to those who believed in his name,
he gave the right to become children of God.*
John 1:12

BABY
October 1975
The Lord Has Heard My Weeping

It was the summer after I graduated from high school and my family had moved for the second time in about a year. My parents argued more than ever. My boyfriend was visiting, and we went out to celebrate his birthday. I had missed him and was deeply affected by the strained relationships at home, so I gave into his advances that night. I lost my virginity and became pregnant at the same time. How could this happen to me? I was a *good girl*. I could start over if only I weren't pregnant.

Only one way could make that happen. Now that abortion was legal, I wouldn't have to drive out of state to take care of my problem. No one would ever need to know. I convinced my boyfriend that it was the best solution, but it wasn't as easy as I thought it would be. While I was on the table having the abortion procedure, I finally realized what I was doing. I cried out for the doctor to stop, but he said it was too late. I sobbed for my mother as I lay in the recovery area. I prayed but was certain that God would never forgive me for what I had done.

My first reaction? Bury the pain. So I drank, smoked, got high, and had sex because nothing mattered any more. I was on my way to hell anyway. I wasn't searching for happiness, just numbness.

After two years of misdirected living, I timidly entered my mother's church. I returned each week and began to hope that God could forgive me. Recovery came in stages. First, I accepted God's forgiveness through His Son's death on the cross, but did not fully grasp what that meant.

After I married and was expecting my first child, I began experiencing flashbacks, nightmares, and anxiety associated with post-abortion syndrome. The reality that I had snuffed out a baby's life struck me with fresh intensity. In horror and despair, I went to God again for His forgiving love. Yet, though I spoke of receiving His love for me, I had difficulty bonding with my little girl.

After my second child was born, I sensed the isolation I had brought on myself due to a damaged relationship with my husband and children. I sought the help of a Christian counselor who led me to the cross time and time again to lay it all before the Lord. I finally experienced His love for me in a life-changing way. The burden of my abortion was lifted, and I was free to give back to the Lord by volunteering at our local crisis pregnancy center. Soon the center hired me to counsel other post-abortion women.

Recently, while attending classes on starting a post-abortion support group, I noticed a display of the National Memorial for the Unborn. At first, I avoided a close look at this display, and asked the Lord if I had an unresolved issue. Gently He revealed to me that I had never grieved the loss of my baby, and that I didn't feel I had a right to grieve since I was the one who caused its death. As I imagined placing my own plaque at The Memorial, my tears flowed, and God's healing love washed over me. That day I went to the display and spoke to the woman representing The Memorial. We hugged and I cried as I told her of my experience and my desire to place a memorial plaque. I am pleased that my baby can be remembered with the dignity due a human life. My family now can remember the one who died too soon. The plaque reads, "The Lord has heard my weeping" from Psalm 6, because truly He has heard and has been my comfort and healing.

—Anonymous

The Lord has heard my weeping.
The Lord has heard my cry for mercy.
Psalm 6:8, 9

BABY ANGEL LUTHER
Autumn 1996
Mark 10:14

My story is different since I am the grandmother in this situation, and my daughter chose to have an abortion. I personally did not agreed with her decision, yet I did not condemn my daughter for her choice. My heart cries often for that precious life that I now believe is with our Lord in heaven. No one knows of my placing a plaque at this Memorial for my lost grandchild. It is my secret gift to him or her. Eleven years ago, I too faced the frightening future of pregnancy without the support of the father or my own family. I stood up to all the odds and my parents disowned me, and the father walked out of my life. I gave birth to identical twin boys, who are the blessings of all our lives now. I cannot imagine life without them. I trusted in the Lord who cares for all His little children.

My daughter chose another road, and I hope she will be okay. I will always cry for that precious life I will never know down here. This small gift of a memorial is all I can do other than pray.

—Anonymous

> *[Jesus] said to them, "Let the children come to me, and do not hinder them, for the kingdom of God belongs to such as these."*
> Mark 10:14

BABY JAMIE DEARMAN
February 1991
I Loved You Too Late

I was 21 years old when I had my abortion. I was in love with a man who abused me emotionally. I didn't recognize the relationship as abusive because of my own insecurities and need for attention.

When I became pregnant, the relationship ended. I pleaded with my boyfriend to stand by me through the pregnancy because I did not believe in abortion. He told me to have an abortion because no one would marry me with someone else's child. I was devastated, desperate, and all alone.

For three months, I thought about how I would get through this. I turned to my close friends, and they only had mixed answers. I knew I would have to tell my parents eventually because I lived under their roof. I could not make it alone in Hawaii, considering the high cost of living. I waited for the right moment to tell my mother, hoping she would be more sympathetic than my dad.

The response I got was devastating, especially from a Christian. My mother told me I would be homeless, and they would not help me through this terrible sin I committed. I said, "Then I'll have to have an abortion . . ." She didn't respond or try to stop me. I felt that this was the last straw, and I would have to go through with it. I wished she had encouraged me to keep the child and assured me that I would not be alone.

That afternoon, my best friend and I went to the clinic for my abortion. During the whole procedure, I wailed in agony and despair. Afterwards, I felt relief and went into a period of denial. I did not allow myself to think that I had murdered a baby. I thought of it as just a ball of cells.

For three years, I was in denial. By then, I was married and had a son. Memories of that terrible day often swept over me at night. I knew I had taken a life, and I didn't think Jesus would forgive me. At the time, I knew what the Bible said, and I still went through with the abortion. Taking a post-abortion class with other women was helpful, for I found others just like me. We learned that no sin was too great for Christ's mercy and forgiveness. I now have solid confidence that I am a forgiven sinner because Christ loved me enough to help me find Him again.

Although I'm forgiven, I'll never satisfy my desire to know what my child looked like or what kind of personality he or she had. Placing a plaque for my child at The Memorial began a period of hope. Now I have given the child an identity, and a place to be recognized as a real person.

—Sue Ann Schumacher

"This is the covenant I will make with them after that time, says the Lord. I will put my laws in their hearts, and I will write them on their minds." Then he adds: "Their sins and lawless acts I will remember no more."
Hebrews 10:16, 17

BABY M
May 15, 1979
A Part of Our Hearts

I had an abortion on May 15, 1979. I was in my junior year at Oregon State University and dating my boyfriend who is now my husband. When I discovered I was pregnant, I couldn't believe it. That would never happen to me . . . I was going to finish school, get married, and have children when I was ready. I never considered following through with the pregnancy. John suggested we get married and keep the baby. I wanted to wait and do it right. I counseled with a woman at a Planned Parenthood clinic and told her that I wanted an abortion. She gave me a list of abortion clinics; I chose the least expensive one. I did ask her about the development of the fetus, and she told me it was just tissue at that point. John and I drove to Vancouver, Washington, on a beautiful May morning. I filled out the necessary paperwork and was ushered into a sterile room for the procedure. I was so embarrassed and wanted the whole thing over with so I could get on with my life.

The abortion wasn't physically painful, but I was surprised by my emotions—I could not stop crying. Tears rolled down my face the whole morning and I didn't know why. I wanted this abortion; I was glad I didn't have to have a baby when I wasn't ready.

I met John in the waiting room when it was over, and he asked, "Why the tears?" I laughed it off. We went to McDonald's for breakfast and drove back to college. We never discussed the abortion. It was over. I soon forgot this ever happened and I went on with my life.

When our third child was born in 1990, my husband John and I were new Christians. Everything was going great. One child was in kindergarten and the other was in second grade. One afternoon while I sat rocking Daniel, the realization of what I had done hit me. I cried, wiped my tears, and went on with my duties as wife and mother.

When Daniel was two, I knew I needed to tell a friend about the abortion if I was to continue to grow as a person and a follower of Jesus Christ. She accepted me, cried with me, and loved me. Later, as grief rolled over me, I couldn't stop the flow of tears. I cried every day, all day, even in the middle of the night. I finally sought professional counseling to deal with the fact that I had killed one of my babies.

Now I realize that God has forgiven me. Jesus' death on the cross can rescue us no matter what we have done. He loves me and holds my baby in heaven at this time. How I long for the day to be reunited with the child I love. I wonder if it is a boy or a girl and if it has blue eyes like the other three. I am so sorry for what I did. How I wish I could undo what I have done, but I can't and I live with the consequences of my actions.

For four years, I have been working through the pain of choosing that abortion. I am in a group with other women who regret their decisions to have abortions. My husband and I still cannot discuss it; it is too painful for us.

I am grateful there is a place where my baby is memorialized. I would love to visit the National Memorial for the Unborn and see the plaque on The Wall for my baby.

—Patti M.

[Jesus] called the crowd to him along with his disciples and said: "If anyone would come after me, he must deny himself and take up his cross and follow me. For whoever wants to save his life will lose it, but whoever loses his life for me and for the gospel will save it."
Mark 8:34, 35

CAROL GAYLE NIEHAUS
July 11, 1984
Psalm 51:1-17

Out of guilt and affection, I slept with someone I had known for several years. It only happened once, but it was enough.

Looking back, I never really considered anything other than abortion. No one tried to suggest anything else, especially the father, who couldn't have cared less. Only one person tried to persuade me to have the baby, but I shrugged her off. I was sick as a dog, and I just wanted to feel better. I also wanted to protect my dad (my mother died when I was nine). It would have hurt him so deeply. Since abortion was legal, I assumed it was okay.

Believe it or not, I was cheerful before, during, and after the abortion and was naive enough to tell several people about it. I considered children a nuisance and wondered why everyone didn't have abortions to get rid of the noisy things. I was very pro-choice.

During this time I faithfully attended church but was not walking with the Lord. In fact, I disdained real believers. I had never heard a sermon against abortion. No one said it was wrong. But about eight years later, I watched a massive Pro-Life demonstration in Wichita, Kansas, on TV when I suddenly realized I agreed with what they said. My heart broke when I realized what I had done. When friends told me they were praying for me because of my liberal attitudes, I thought that wasn't fair. Later, I was grateful for those prayers that started my grieving process. I killed my baby out of ignorance, and I will not live a lie any longer.

Having my child's plaque at the National Memorial for the Unborn has given me peace of mind to know that others remember my baby. Thank you for this chance to come clean.

—Debbie Niehaus

*Wash away all my iniquity
and cleanse me from my sin.*
Psalm 51:2

*Be joyful always; pray continually;
give thanks in all circumstances, for this
is God's will for you in Christ Jesus.*
1 Thessalonians 5:16–18

CRYSTAL STARR STRUBE
Brightest Star in Heaven

My ex-husband and I decided to abort our third child because of the instability of our marriage, our finances, and our desires. We saw what our problems were doing to our other two children. Instead of seeking counsel, we chose to abort and give up. Little did we know what we would deal with the rest of our lives.

During my abortion I actually saw an innocent life ripped apart and trashed like garbage. The ordeal was enough to put me to bed weeping for days. To deal with the pain, I turned to drugs and alcohol. My first marriage disintegrated quickly, and I married two more times. I tried everything to ease the pain of what I thought was insanity.

Several years in denial went by before God finally got my attention. I was literally on the edge and suicide seemed the only way out. Being a Christian, I knew I needed help. That is when I began to deal with the tragedy that haunted the inner depths of my very soul. Healing has not been an easy process. But I found peace with God and in myself by forgiving and accepting His forgiveness.

As my healing progressed, I named my baby Crystal Starr and placed my plaque on the Memorial Wall. That was the hardest part of my healing, but I had to get past the pain in order to move onward in life and in God's love. He is faithful to forgive. We just have to learn to forgive ourselves.

—Cynthia Hardeman

I sought the Lord and he answered me; he delivered me from all my fears. Those who look to him are radiant; their faces are never covered with shame.

Psalm 34:4, 5

> **CYNTHIA ANN DUFFIELD**
> September 11, 1990
> *In Loving Memory*

In August 1990, when I was forty-three, my husband of twenty-three years and I sat in our business office contemplating the green positive pregnancy strip in disbelief. At the time, our family consisted of a sixteen-year-old daughter and a thirteen-year old son. We considered what it would mean to our already stressed marriage to have another child like our severely retarded son. Three different physicians told us the odds were against us and advised us to abort. Our faith was not well grounded, and we were frightened beyond belief. Rather than treasuring the child as a gift and acknowledging God's sovereignty, we assumed the baby would be like our son. Neither one of us could imagine rearing two handicapped children.

Having worked for a physician for fourteen years who performed abortions, I looked at these girls with pity, thinking I'd never be one of them. Now I was standing in their shoes. The short-term effect of my abortion experience was far more devastating than I anticipated. I bought the lie that says once the "procedure" is done, all would be back to normal. Instead, I felt an overwhelming sense of loss. My arms ached for the child I would never hold. I kept focusing on the remains of my child and remembering the tissue results on the pathology report reading: PRODUCTS OF CONCEPTION. It had always been another woman's problem. Now it was mine.

As the days became months, I thought time would heal my wound, my shame, but it didn't. I confided in a friend who referred me to a post-abortion program in 1994. Finally, my very controlled self lost control, and I wept for my loss and my family's loss. Through the class, God's Word introduced me to my child. I was able to acknowledge my sin, to say hello to my daughter, and ask her to forgive me for what her father and I had done.

It has meant so much to both my husband and me to acknowledge our child by memorializing her at the National Memorial for the Unborn. We have promised her that we will fight for the rights of the unborn to honor her memory. We are joyful at the prospect of seeing her when we are all with the Lord. She is no longer in my heart as a secret and painful event but rather as my treasured child, just as I treasure both her brother and sister.

—Laurie Duffield

For I am the LORD, your God, who takes
hold of your right hand and says to you,
Do not fear; I will help you.
Isaiah 41:13

DANIEL CALEB ALVERSON
January 1970
A Bud on Earth Blooms in Heaven

I felt as if I was in a dream. This couldn't really be happening to me, could it? In 1969, as a junior at the University of Kansas, I was home to celebrate the Christmas holidays with my family in Michigan. But something was wrong—very wrong. My period was two weeks late, and now even the thought of food, let alone the smell or taste of it, nauseated me. "I just can't be pregnant!" I kept thinking. Not now, with only a year and a half left before I earned my business degree. After all, Jim and I had sex only a couple of times.

When I returned to school, the test at the university clinic only proved what I already knew. I was twenty years old, unmarried, and pregnant. I did not know the Lord, but I tried to be a good person. With no firm foundation to stand on, I was floundering. Even though I intended to wait until I was married to have sex, I gave in to tremendous pressure and ended up in a frightening situation to me. When I found out I was pregnant, I sobbed for a day, then pulled myself together enough to think the situation through. Since Jim and I were only friends, marriage was out of the question. Abortion was generally illegal in the United States at that time, so I decided to have my baby and put it up for adoption. I would miss only one semester of school and could start again in the fall after the baby was born. I hoped my brother in Colorado would provide a place to stay for the summer months before the baby was born. It wasn't long, however, before I discovered that others, eager to help, had another plan.

First, my minister at my home church gave my family details for obtaining a legal abortion in England. Then my roommate told me how to obtain a legal abortion right there in Kansas. Her father, a physician, would help me get the necessary papers.

So it was decided that I would have an abortion at the university medical center. *This must be the best decision,* I thought. *My parents, my brother, my roommate, a physician, Jim, and even the minister all think this will be an easy, quick solution to a difficult problem,* I reasoned. *As soon as it's over, I can forget about it and get on with my life.* I would discover how wrong I was.

I returned home to my apartment eager to start the new semester. Jim and I were still friendly, but we never went out again nor did we mention the abortion. Something strange was happening to me, though. I kept feeling this intense desire to be a mother. *What is wrong with me?* I asked myself. *I don't want to be pregnant and have a baby out of wedlock!* As I tried to decipher these strange thoughts, I felt almost a physical pain that intensified into severe physical pain.

At the clinic, the doctors decided a spastic colon was causing the pain, most likely a result of the stress of the abortion and resulting mourning for the aborted baby. I remained in the hospital two weeks before I was released. Since I missed two weeks of the semester and was in a weakened condition, I decided to go home. I was relieved to get away from that place and immediately felt better once I left. It was easier to put everything behind me without all the familiar reminders.

In the fall, I returned to school to resume my education. The spastic colon surfaced again as the memories returned, but I got into the swing of things and began doing just fine, although the abortion was not far from my thoughts. I met Larry Alverson in one of my business classes, and after our first date on November 3, 1970, we were inseparable. I went home for Christmas vacation once again, but this time I was exuberant with news of my engagement. What a difference from the previous year!

Larry and I were married the following August, and since I would graduate in December, we decided to try to have a baby soon after we returned from our honeymoon. I would finally be able to satisfy the inexplicable yearning I had experienced ever since the abortion. One year went by. Then two years became three years, and still no pregnancy. We finally went to the doctor for infertility testing. After several procedures, it was discovered that a mild infection from the abortion had caused a blockage in my Fallopian tubes. I underwent surgery at the University of Michigan Medical Center to correct the problem.

Two more years went by. Then late one night I awoke in such horrible pain that I could not sit up. Larry turned the light on to see his wife looking as white as the sheets. He rushed me to the hospital where my blood pressure was discovered to be 60/40 and dropping. Emergency surgery was performed, and my right tube and ovary were removed. I had experienced an ectopic pregnancy due to scar tissue from the abortion and previous surgery. The Fallopian tube burst as the baby grew too large for it to contain. I would have bled to death had Larry not responded so quickly to the situation. In order to avoid another ectopic pregnancy and possible death, I had a third major surgery to repair my remaining tube six months later. That was in 1977 and I have never become pregnant again.

Dealing with all of this was complicated by something else that happened not long before we started the infertility testing. One year after Larry and I were married, we were wonderfully born again. It felt so good to be cleansed and forgiven of all my past! I had specifically asked forgiveness for the abortion, but I still had a vague feeling that it was wrong, and I did not really understand its impact upon my life. One day I was talking with my best friend, Georgianna, who was also my first close Christian friend. We were discussing the excitement of her first pregnancy. During the course of our conversation, I told Georgianna, who is a nurse, about my abortion. She asked me how far along I had been at the time and I told her almost eleven weeks.

She looked at me and said so gently, "Averie, did you know that your baby was already completely formed, already had fingernails and toenails? All it had left to do was grow."

At that moment I experienced shock and horror! "You mean it wasn't just a mass of tissue like I was led to believe?" I agonized. I felt like a huge knife was shoved into my stomach. What had I done? I realized for the first time what all those unexplained feelings meant. It took me many years after that to deal with the infertility and the guilt of abortion. I could not have made it through so beautifully and victoriously had it not been for our wonderful heavenly Father and His Word. No one talked about abortion then, and post-abortion trauma had never been heard of, so it was just me and the Lord quietly working through this together. Because of the complication of infertility, Satan was eager to heap guilt and condemnation upon me, but fortunately, I knew God's Word said my sin had been removed from me as far as the east is from the west. I will always regret my decision to have an abortion, but I do not have to carry a heavy load of guilt for it anymore.

    Although I had found true peace inside, I was still bothered by the world's seeming ignorance about post-abortion stress and trauma. So when I heard in 1991 that sponsors of Informed Consent Legislation in the Michigan legislature were looking for women who had experienced an abortion to testify about the advisability of such legislation, I immediately volunteered. I then gave my testimony before about 1,500 people at our church in 1992 to help the church learn how to reach out to these hurting women with love, hope, and healing. Next, I began post-abortion support groups for women in our church and community.

    As a result of leading the support groups, I received further healing for my own abortion, especially at the memorial service we held for our babies. You see, when you have an abortion, you want to deny that your baby exists, and you don't want anyone to know about him. The memorial service was one way I could recognize my child was a real person with a name and an identity, and restore to him the dignity that I had taken from him when I decided to end his life. When I heard about the National Memorial for the Unborn, I knew right away that I wanted Daniel's name to be on The Wall. It was the final thing I could do for him. I am so thankful for a beautiful place where others can remember him.

—Averie Alverson

As far as the east is from the west, so far has he removed our transgressions from us. As a father has compassion on his children, so the Lord *has compassion on those who fear him.*
Psalm 103:12, 13

DAVID ANDREW PAINE
1978
I'm sorry I hurt you. Forgive me.

In 1978, I was a young woman married and deeply in love with my husband. When I discovered I was pregnant, he was unemployed and I had only a part-time job. His sister and her three children were living with us, and she had no money and no ambition. She, the kids, and my husband watched TV while I was at work, and they left the housework and yard work to me. This put a tremendous strain on our marriage. I realized that my husband was lazy and unconcerned about our future. As I watched the interactions between these children and their mother, I tried to see myself in the role as a mother. The idea of bringing a child into this atmosphere frightened me. I wanted our home in good order when a child came.

When I told a friend I was considering abortion, he became angry and told me how wrong it was. We argued. But I knew abortion was an option for me, and I loved having that choice. It gave me power over my life. I talked to a supportive girlfriend who offered to go with me to the clinic. My husband said he didn't care, and would let me decide. This was his way of avoiding the responsibility.

I then tried to kill the baby by drinking heavily and smoking pot. This was my way of totally absolving myself of any wrongdoing. I could tell people, "The poor baby just couldn't live in mommy's tummy, and it died." Then I would get sympathy. But the baby did not die, and I began to feel and see the changes in my body. I made the appointment and asked my friend to go with me. My mind was made up. I was eleven weeks into the pregnancy.

No one provided any information for another choice. No one spoke of the long-term effects or about taking responsibility. This only served to intensify my resolve that it was the right thing for me. I was not influenced by any one person but by the society and the culture I lived in. I was in favor of legalized abortion, I supported the women's movement, I was selfish, and I was in denial. I had a partner who was unwilling to take charge and assure me of his desire to be a daddy. I had all of the key ingredients needed to think that I was making the right decision for myself. I never considered the needs of the child.

At my gynecologist's office, the procedure was commonplace—I know, because I had seen the brochures and posters on the walls on previous visits. It felt safe because he was my doctor. Afterwards, my life took a downward turn, but I didn't know it was related to the abortion. I can only see that now. I got divorced and involved with another man right away, and he became cruel and abusive. I started to drink excessively and spent a lot of time crying. I wanted to die and even planned my suicide. But the Lord intervened in my life in a miraculous way and gave me the courage to face the truth of how awful my life was. When I stopped living in denial, I came to terms with the fact that I had killed my child. It was the only child I have ever conceived, so today I am childless.

God has allowed me to see that if I had not aborted that baby, perhaps the child would have been the incentive my husband needed to help him grow up and assume responsibility as the head of our home. By aborting the baby, I denied him that role, cheating both of us from possibly staying married and having more children. In playing God, making life and death decisions that are His alone, I destroyed more lives than just the one.

Giving my child a name and placing a plaque at the National Memorial for the Unborn has brought me peace. It gave me the opportunity to say to the world that I made a choice that ended my own child's life. What a statement! If every aborted child's name were listed somewhere in print, perhaps the people of this country would wake up to the pure evil of abortion.

I look forward to heaven where I can hold my child, look into his eyes, and tell him "I'm sorry I hurt you."

—Rosalie DiMaggio

But God demonstrates his own love for us in this:
While we were still sinners, Christ died for us.
Romans 5:8

ENOCH AND NATHANEL
February 14th
Clay in the Potter's Hands

My name is Brenda Darnell, and I am an abortionist! You may think that I have overreacted to make such a statement about an event that happened only once in my life, but for thirty-three years, I have lived and relived this event in my heart, mind, and soul.

I was eleven, the event was rape, and the outcome was a pregnancy. I did not tell anyone about the rape, but as the weeks went by, I became sicker and sicker. Every day at school as I smelled the food cooking in the lunchroom, I had to be excused. After being sick for four months, my mother and I came face-to-face with what happened. The doctor confirmed my *illness,* and the police arrested the rapist and put him in jail. He did time, and I've done life!

When I was five months pregnant, my doctor and mother decided I should have an abortion. At this time, the only places in the United States to have legal abortions were in New York and Colorado. The choice was Colorado, and the hospital stay would be three days. The abortion was done, but because of a mental block, I did not go into labor for two weeks. When I did go into labor, I gave birth to a son. He was black because he'd been dead for two weeks. Then, one-and-one-half hours later while taking a shower, I delivered my second son—twins!

Eleven, raped, pregnant, sick, abortion, twins, death! Nothing in life has brought me more pain, and no eraser is big enough to make my hurt and pain go away.

I have made many wrong choices because I did not feel as if God could ever love or forgive me for taking the lives of my two sons. But I learned that God does love me. He not only has forgiven me but has brought me out of darkness into His light.

Recently, I attended a ten-week Bible study that has changed my whole life and healed my broken heart. I didn't know that other women were suffering the pain of post-abortion trauma. Now as I share my story, I meet women who are also in bondage because of their pasts.

I am thankful for the National Memorial for the Unborn. If you look behind the cross on The Wall of Names, you will see my children's plaque. Those are my sons, and one day I will hold them in heaven.

—Brenda Darnell

But the pot he was shaping from the clay was marred in his hands; so the potter formed it into another pot, shaping it as seemed best to him. . . . Like clay in the hand of the potter, so are you in my hand, O house of Israel.

Jeremiah 18:4, 6

FOR ALL MY CHILDREN
January 1974–July 1980
You Are Now Loved—Psalm 32

I was the perfect candidate for legalized abortion. I was still in high school, and the father of the baby did not want to marry. I was seventeen when I chose my first abortion. I felt pressure from my education. In high school, we were taught about population control, pollution, and the high cost of unwanted children in this world. Feminist teachers said that being a teen mother was low on the ladder of success.

I was afraid to face my parents with the consequences of my actions. Since I was raised in a religious home, I knew abortion was morally wrong. My abortion separated me from my parents and from the God of my youth.

After my abortion, guilt and grief consumed me. I went to counselor after counselor looking for help. They said that women should not feel guilty after doing something that is right for them. I began to use drugs and alcohol in attempts to ease the emotional pain and thought something was wrong with me for not coping. I not only became involved with the feminist movement but chose abortion three more times as I looked for answers to the pain caused by my "right to choose." After the fourth abortion, I went overseas, searching for God in every country I visited.

I married a man I met traveling. We wanted children, but I could not conceive. After two years of trying, I miscarried a baby in the eighth week. The miscarriage brought me to my knees as I cried to God in anguish. I thought I had damaged my body from all the abortions and I would never be able to have another child. Now face-to-face with the preciousness of life, I was ashamed for taking the lives of my own children. I prayed, *God, you took babies from me just like I took them from you. If you will give me a baby, I will give you my life.* Two weeks later, I conceived my whole and healthy daughter. Shortly after, I surrendered my life to Jesus Christ. I was thrilled to find all the emotional help I ever needed in the Bible. I began writing down what I found in His Word. In attending a small group for post-abortive women in our local crisis pregnancy center, I found the comfort and support I needed.

The National Memorial for the Unborn was a precious part of my healing process. It restored dignity to the lives I took and allowed me a public profession of repentance and grief. I will never forget the day I put up a marker for all my children in heaven. God makes all things beautiful in His time, and the National Memorial for the Unborn is something beautiful for Him.

—Linda Cochrane

Against you, you only, have I sinned and done what is evil in your sight . . . Wash me, and I will be whiter than snow.
Psalm 51:4, 7

Many are the woes of the wicked, but the Lord's unfailing love surrounds the man who trusts in him.
Psalm 32:10

HEIDI
February 19, 1973
Alive in My Heart & in Heaven

My second husband and I had a prenuptial agreement that if I became pregnant, I would have an abortion. I agreed because I never expected to be pregnant, but when I found myself pregnant in January 1973, I had to choose between my husband and the baby.

I made the wrong choice and had abortion. The moment the anesthesia wore off, I knew I had killed my baby. It was no longer a glob of tissue. It was a personal part of me—this baby that my body was supposed to nurture and protect. I had murdered it. I never expected to be a murderer. I couldn't share this secret with anyone, except my husband.

My husband didn't understand my grief, my remorse. He simply said we made the best choice. I hated him and wanted to wound him deeply. I wanted him to hurt as I hurt, and I acted out that anger by having an affair. He seemed not to notice, not to care. We soon divorced.

Now I was completely alone and a murderer. I was self-destructive, but I found a way to justify my own abortion. I became deeply involved in the abortion industry and started selling abortions. Each time I sold another woman an abortion, she was okay. If she was okay, then maybe I was okay.

EMPTY ARMS

I made a lot of money in this work. At the end of each day, I counted the number of abortions and multiplied that number times twenty-five dollars to see how much money I had made. Wanting to be a millionaire, I had to do 40,000 abortions to accomplish that. I planned to open five abortion clinics surrounding the Dallas/Ft. Worth area and become a millionaire by 1983.

Then I met a man who offered me something I'd never understood before. He told me that Jesus died on the cross for my sins. If I would accept Him by faith, I could have eternal life. I could be free from the pain of my past. I prayed the sinner's prayer, but I didn't believe it covered the sin of abortion. I thought that was unforgivable. Later, I confessed my sins and experienced God's cleansing and forgiveness.

Now I had to face the fact that I not only killed my daughter, but also a part of me. I had to grieve her death and forgive myself. I named her Heidi, which means *noble*. To me it means *hidden*, for she is hidden from the world but alive in my heart and in heaven.

There is no cemetery where post-aborted women can go to mourn and lay down our grief. But a plaque remembering Heidi is at the National Memorial for the Unborn.

Someday, I am going to see Heidi. For years I wondered what I would say if she asked me why I aborted her. Now I realize that she won't ask that question in heaven. Since there are no tears in heaven, Heidi will rush to meet me and I can hold her for the first time.

—Carol Everett

If we confess our sins he is faithful and just and will forgive us our sins and purify us from all unrighteousness.
1 John 1:9

> **JEREMY RUSSELL**
> November 1979
> *Home Free—John 8:32*

Since I was the eldest of three children, my parents expected me to be the perfect example for my brother and sister. They worked to provide for us, and we attended church on Sundays. I had little interest in boys, was uncomfortable with my sexuality, and was having fun with my girlfriends.

That all changed when I met Steve. Within two years, something I never thought would happen to me did. At age nineteen, I lived at home, attended a local college, and became pregnant. When I told my parents they took me to an abortion clinic, and I aborted an eight-week baby (a blob of tissue, I thought). My parents and I never discussed the abortion and life went on. End of problem, right? No way!

Eventually, I ended up in a loving Christian counselor's office, working through many problems—codependency, bulimia, divorce. With all this behind me, I remarried in 1991. In March of 1993, I discovered that I was pregnant again. The following December, God gave us a perfect little daughter. I was overwhelmed with joy mixed with sorrow for the baby I had aborted fourteen years earlier. Whenever I looked at Holly, I remembered what I had done to an innocent unborn child. Yes, it was a baby, not a blob of tissue. I tried desperately to forget but was unsuccessful. I later learned that what

I thought was postpartum depression was really post-abortion depression.

In February of 1995, a friend gave me a copy of *Something Better News* where I saw an advertisement for a post-abortion organization. I called the next day to get more information and was invited to a post-abortion Bible study support group. I knew I was free from my past sins, but I hadn't dealt with the guilt and shame I carried around from my abortion. Through the Bible study, I learned that I am responsible for what I did but now I am completely forgiven and free from the guilt and shame I carried for so long.

The world would have you believe that a fetus is just a blob of tissue, but the truth is that life begins at conception. My abortion not only killed an innocent baby, but it also wounded me physically and emotionally. For many years, I wondered what was wrong with me until finally, through this Bible study and the other women in my support group, God healed me from those deep wounds and set me free from the pain of abortion.

My son's plaque at The Memorial acknowledges his life. Now he has a place of significance and dignity for all the world to see. These plaques signify hope for others who have had abortions. They also give hope to those facing crisis pregnancies, who might save their unborn children and themselves from pain. Jeremy is gone to be with Jesus, but he will never be forgotten. The Memorial is a true blessing!

—Sherri Madill

Then you will know the truth, and the truth will set you free.
John 8:32

JESSE HAWTHORNE BARE
September 1981
"Redeemed"

One day in 1992 I was driving to my post-abortion counseling Bible study when I asked the Lord to help me name my aborted son. I seemed to sense God saying to me, *Your baby has been in heaven for over eleven years. Don't you think we've named him by now?* The name "Jesse" came to mind. Excitedly, I claimed this name for the child I would never hold this side of heaven.

With the first name selected, work on the last name became my focus. I struggled with giving Jesse his father's last name as he would probably never acknowledge our son, but my maiden name didn't seem right either.

Out of the blue I received a call from my ex-boyfriend's father, the baby's grandfather. I had written to him two years earlier asking for forgiveness, but he had never responded. Now he called to say that he and his wife had forgiven me and were proud of my Pro-Life efforts. They loved our child greatly, he said.

When I hung up the phone, I knew that Jesse's name was complete. Because of his grandfather's love for him, Jesse would have his last name. Now I could finally order his plaque for the National Memorial for the Unborn.

EMPTY ARMS

It took me years to name Jesse, but I'm confident that God named him long ago as He cared for him in heaven. How wonderful to realize that Jesus is the greatest parent a child could ever have.

Later, the first child God would ever use me to save from abortion would bear the name Jesse. His mother didn't know my child's name but God did. He gave me that experience to have a living reminder that He knew my baby, and He would redeem my mistake to point others to the choice of life.

—Sydna Masse

The nations will see your righteousness, and all kings your glory; you will be called by a new name that the mouth of the Lord will bestow.

Isaiah 62:2

JESSICA RENEE
December 6, 1992
My Silent Inspiration

I was raised in a wonderful Christian family. In fact, my father was the youth minister of the small Baptist church we attended. You can imagine the anxiety I felt after realizing I might be pregnant.

I went to a crisis pregnancy center alone to settle my suspicion. I remember thinking as I waited for my test results, *This is not the way it happened in my dreams.* The test confirmed my worst nightmare. But somehow, in the midst of all my fear and regret, I felt excited. I was going to have a baby! I thought of all the events that would follow as a little heartbeat—silent and unnoticed yet full of life—grew stronger inside me.

The days that followed were the worst of my life. When I told the baby's father, he reminded me that he was going to a major university, and this "little inconvenience" was mine. The next step was to tell my parents. I will never forget the expressions on their faces as I revealed my problem. *They went into emotional overload with an urgent need to fix this problem.* We made a life-changing decision for all involved, especially for that silent heartbeat that had become a lullaby to my soul.

A week after telling my parents of my pregnancy, I had an abortion. My entire world collapsed around me, leaving me numb. As I shut off all emotions, no life was left in me—not even the beautiful little heart beating only moments before. The days and weeks that followed were filled with hate and misery. I honestly felt I was losing my mind. All I could think about was the horrible thing I had done and the cold truth that I would live with the reality of that decision every day of my life. As I continued to self-destruct, I knew my only hope was to return to the Lord. I remembered feeling safe with Him, and I wanted to find my way back to Him, but He seemed so far away.

I heard about a Bible study for post-abortive women held, ironically, at the same crisis pregnancy center (CPC) that had given me my pregnancy test. As I began the class I felt as if nothing could take away this pain. Then I came face-to-face with the truth, and Jesus Christ became my lifeboat. It was not easy, but He gently pulled me back into His presence. I am thankful that He is a God of the trenches. He came into my trench of sin and lifted me out. As I struggled to deal with my decision and myself, He cleansed me of all unrighteousness. He truly is my Savior, Lord, Father, and best Friend.

Truth. What an all-encompassing word. As I learned the truth about the way Christ felt about me, I realized another truth: I had taken the life of my baby. I was broken before the Lord and wept for my baby girl, Jessie. At the end of the Bible study sessions we had a memorial service for our babies. For the first time, I acknowledged the life of Jessie Renee. My life changed that day. I dedicated myself to doing everything in my power to keep this from happening to other women and children. My heavenly Father became the strength behind that decision, and Jessie became my inspiration.

I am now a site director for a branch of that same CPC and attended the dedication service for the National Memorial for the Unborn. That was such a beautiful experience. I had the honor of placing my daughter's nameplate on The Wall. Her plaque is in the shadow of the cross where my life is also. I realized that day that my *little inconvenience,* my *worst nightmare,* my *problem* was none of those things. She was my precious baby Jessie, who in her very short lifetime changed mine. I never had the hospital gown with her handprints on it, but she left her handprints on my heart.

I love you, Jessie.

—Candy Little

But when he, the Spirit of truth, comes, he will
guide you into all truth. He will not speak on his own;
he will speak only what he hears, and he will
tell you what is yet to come.
John 16:13

JONATHAN DAVID
Spring 1978
We Hold You in Our Hearts

Personal choices have immense ramifications, but the choices others make can affect our lives, too, especially when we are children.

I grew up in a so-called Christian home where incest was rampant. My grandfather raped me for the first time when I was six years old. He also sat me in his lap at church every Sunday. Other family members abused me as well. This abuse dealt a severe blow to my ability to trust and shattered my fragile concept of God.

When my parents became missionaries and we moved overseas, the abuse should have ceased. But secrets carry heavy price tags. When I was twelve a youth/music minister in his early twenties offered to teach me guitar lessons. My parents readily agreed for his church position was all the credential they needed. Soon the music lessons turned into rape sessions. My past history of abuse increased my vulnerability.

Surprisingly, I conceived. But an unmarried pregnant daughter would have forced my parents off the mission field, and they were trapped. They had taught me to value life. Yet when they took me to the doctor to confirm pregnancy, they conspired with him to perform a chemical abortion. They told me that they didn't know if I was pregnant or not but the pills would cause me no harm if I were. I celebrated the day my baby died, thinking my period had started. Soon I was put in the hospital with a severe uterine infection. Naively, I didn't put the pieces together until much later—much too late to save my baby.

Denial is a powerful force. I minimized the effects of the years of abuse. It wasn't until I had been married nine years and had given birth to three children that the damage surfaced. I became agoraphobic, feeling helpless in an inescapable situation. This frightening condition forced me to seek help. I began counseling, dealing exclusively with the abuse issues. During the next three years, I worked diligently to overcome the pain and rejection left by the abuse. Layer after layer was exposed. I had begun to stabilize when the abortion surfaced. The truth was revealed when I began having horrendous nightmares and realized the abortion was at the core of my psychological problems. With the help of my counselor and a post-abortive counselor, I was able to put the pieces together.

The abortion has greatly affected every area of my life. I've battled suicide, longing for the intense pain to end. I couldn't save myself from the abuse and rape. I couldn't save my baby from the abortion. Powerlessness overwhelmed me. Guilt plagued me. Emptiness consumed me as the realization hit that I wouldn't see or hold him this side of heaven.

The price I was paying filtered to my husband and children. My husband was forced to become mom and dad while I drowned in sorrow. Financial burdens were added, as I was unable to provide an income. Our finances had never been stable due to my intense desire to have children, regardless of an inadequate income in an effort to replace my lost baby.

As a result, I wasn't able to love my children as themselves. I placed unrealistic expectations on them, wanting them to fill the void left in my heart from the abortion. The children also had to deal with my grief but were not able to comprehend the depth of my sorrow. Abortion robbed holidays and birthdays from us as well. When my oldest turned eleven, I was in a puddle of tears over the other child who would never have a birthday, would never have a cake, or open gifts. I cried that whole day. Childhood should be peaceful and carefree, not riddled with the magnitude of abortion's grief.

Healing has come by others choosing to involve themselves with my grief. Gratitude goes first to Christ. He chose to pay the ultimate price for my healing, spiritually and emotionally. He also held my hand and walked me through this pain. He provided me with a caring husband, a lovely Christian counselor, a post-abortive counselor, and the director of Focus on the Family's Crisis Pregnancy Ministry (she directed me to the National Memorial for the Unborn).

Words can't express what it has meant to me to place a plaque on The Wall. It has helped to restore my dignity. My baby's dignity was restored when he was ushered into Christ's arms. The Memorial is a beacon of love to those of us who have experienced abortion, providing a place of caring. They care that my baby died, and they acknowledge my need for a place to grieve. When my family visited The Memorial to place Jonathan David's plaque on The Wall, we were surrounded by tender loving care. It was heartwarming to know that we weren't alone.

This is how I described the injustice done to my baby:

Absolutely inexcusable,
Babies ripped from our very hearts,
Open arms that can never be filled.
Right to life denied.
This action's injustice rings clear.
Is your reputation and name worth the price we paid?
Only if you had given us the choice and support.
Never can you replace the loss we now face.

People argue that in the face of rape and incest, abortion is not only acceptable but kind. Having lived through all three, I know firsthand that abortion was far more damaging than abuse or rape. Had I been given the choice even of adoption, I wouldn't be dealing with the death of a child. My life was at risk because the abortion's pain pushed me toward full-blown anorexia. In the attempt to spare me through abortion, I was almost consumed. What is more final than death? The belief is that it would be cruel to force a child to carry a baby conceived in violence. I have found the opposite to be true. The abortion didn't relieve the pain of rape and incest. Rather, abortion intensified my pain. The day my baby died, a part of me died with him. I'm left with the pain.

During my grieving process, I wrote letters to my aborted baby. My final letter sums up my motivation to continue toward healing:

Dear Jonathan David,

I search for a way to make sense of your death. It was senseless to me. Yes, it saved the reputation of my parents. It saved the reputation of your father, the man who supposedly represented God, yet thought nothing of raping me repeatedly. Their reputations weren't worth the price we paid.

God has given me a channel to make sense of this chaos—my writing. If our story can save one child, if I can expose the lie that abortion is acceptable in the case of rape and incest, convince one person that it harms victims and sentences them to a lifetime of pain, then I will feel there is purpose. If only one girl is spared my agony, then it's worth it. Your brief earthly existence had a purpose. Know that I love you. Mom

—Julie Crockett

There is a way that seems right to a man, but in the end it leads to death . . . The fear of the Lord *is a fountain of life, turning a man from the snares of death.*
Proverbs 14:12, 27

> # JOSHUA
> June 25, 1988
> *My First Child, I Miss You—Mom*
>
>

Dear Joshua,

We've been asked to share our story, yours and mine, son. Part of me wants to hide it from the world, for I still feel ashamed for what I did to you or didn't do for you. But I know that in sharing our story, you live on, and this compels me to write. I know that you, too, would want me to share it in order to save others from the pain we have both endured.

You are remembered, Joshua. I have placed a plaque in your memory. For so many years after your death, I longed for a way to remember you and for this cold, callous world to remember you with me. When I learned of The Memorial, my heart leapt for joy as you must have leapt within my womb for the thirteen weeks I allowed you to live, hearing my heartbeat. Isn't it ironic, son? My heart of love for your father led to your conception. My heart of fear led to your destruction. Can both reside in one heart at the same time? Jesus said that perfect love drives out fear. I did not love you perfectly, but I did love you. Have you been watching me, son? Did you see the roses I left in front of the clinic doors in your memory? Did you see the birthday cards I have sent each year to the clinic where you died? Some would think I am crazy. I just know that I love you, and losing you made me crazy with grief and sorrow. No one talked with me about you. I remember you in the silence of my heart. There, in my heart, was your funeral and grave, the only place I could find to remember you until now. Yes, I wanted you, son, but your grandmother convinced me not to have you. I have forgiven her, as I know that you've forgiven me.

Did you see me give birth to your brother Michael? He was—*the you*—I had wanted. After my abortion, I longed for another child to replace my empty womb. Michael came, and I fought to allow him to be born. Then, after nine months of love and care, I entrusted your brother into the care of a family who could give him all that he deserved. He erased the shame and sense of guilt that dripped from me daily for two years as a leaky faucet dripping water. But he was no more of a gift than you, my first son.

Your father and I never got married as we had planned. With your death came new life in Christ for me. Did you see me standing in front of the church as *Amazing Grace* played loudly? Did you see my tears? They were for you. It's all been for you, my son. My life changed forever with you. I have never been the same. I hope that I've made you proud, my son.

—Marlena Moore

There is no fear in love. But perfect love drives out fear, because fear has to do with punishment . . . We love because he first loved us.
1 John 4:18, 19

KATIE LUCY SWILLING
August 15, 1973
I'll Hold You in Heaven

When I was fifteen years old, I was sexually active with my boyfriend and became pregnant. The year was 1973, and abortion was now legal. My mother took me to the doctor because I wasn't feeling well. They did a pregnancy test, and it came back positive. Although we didn't discuss the matter, she decided I would have an abortion. I believed it wasn't a baby yet until I could feel it move.

My parents took me to a hospital in Portland, Oregon. The doctors told me I would be asleep, but I was put into a dreamlike state. The abortion was a horrible nightmare because I was aware of what was going on around me. After it was over, I felt relief. Four weeks later, I started suffering from severe depression and anxiety. Then, I was sick with mono and I lay in bed for about six weeks and asked God to let me die.

As the years went by, I learned to suppress the whole experience in my mind. In 1982, I accepted Christ as my Savior and asked God to forgive me but never went any further. As I grew in my spiritual life, the Holy Spirit kept bringing my abortion into my thoughts. Then I found out about our local crisis pregnancy center and knew God wanted me to be involved. I attended a post-abortion conference and now

I am the Post-Abortion Coordinator for our center and a counselor.

During my healing, I prayed that I would know the sex of my child. One night in a dream, I held three babies. One baby slipped out of my hands into the toilet, and I couldn't get her out. The two children left in my arms were my two living children. The little girl going down the drain was my aborted child. I named her Katie Lucy after my two great grandmas. God led me to memorialize her with a plaque at the National Memorial for the Unborn. Last year, at a post-abortion conference, I visited The Memorial. We had a wonderful service, and it was a blessing to see my child's name on The Wall. God has also blessed me in a special way by putting my child's nameplate on the front of The Memorial brochure. I look forward to the day I will hold my daughter in heaven.

—Dee Dee Swilling

Repent, then, and turn to God, so that your sins may be wiped out, that times of refreshing may come from the Lord.
Acts 3:19

LINDY LEE MILLER
Spring 1980
I Love You, Sweetheart

I was nineteen years old and away from home for the first time when my parents divorced. I did not handle this well and began drinking heavily. During this time, I was not careful in my physical relationship with my girlfriend, and she became pregnant.

My initial reaction was, *I need to get a better job to look after this baby!* Mixed with this thought were others like, *What is my mother going to say? What are other people going to say? Oh well, I'll just have to live with it.*

One day as I talked to my girlfriend, she said, "Your mother believes we need to abort the fetus."

Abort it? I thought to myself, *What are you talking about?* Then I thought, *Well, if my mother said so, we have to do it. Besides, people say it is just a fetus. I guess a fetus isn't a human after all.*

After the abortion was over, I realized in terror that it was too late. The baby was gone, and I couldn't bring it back. I knew deep inside the child had been killed.

A priest told me God forgave me, so I decided to serve this God who would forgive such a horrendous act. In time, He gave me opportunities to be healed internally for my misbehavior. At church I helped with a club ministering to young boys without fathers. Then I helped to raise money for starving children. Now I could tell myself that I was saving children's lives.

After I got married and we were expecting our first child, my wife had a miscarriage. I cried on the way home from work after hearing the news from my wife and when I got home, we cried together. I always wanted to be a father. Our Christian friends were supportive, sending cards, articles, and expressing condolences. Then it dawned on me—it really wasn't a fetus we lost all those years ago—it was a beloved child.

All the pain that I had stuffed inside over the loss of the relationship I could have had with my little aborted child was released. I cried and let out the pain that had been working on my soul for seventeen years.

I also went to counseling regarding the abortion. There the abortion changed from an ugly experience that I was mad and bitter about, to the realization that I had a child in heaven with Jesus. At the end of the counseling sessions, I had a memorial service for my child and placed her in Jesus' care.

My counselor challenged me to contact my old girlfriend and apologize to her for not being man enough to stop her from going for the abortion. I did this and felt like another monkey had come off my back.

I shared these experiences with a women's post-abortion support group. When the floor was open for questions, someone commented that I must have had hard feelings toward my mother for telling my girlfriend to have an abortion. Someone else asked if I had talked to her about it. I said I hadn't. Later, I asked my mother if she had indeed influenced my girlfriend in that way. She said she had not. It was a relief to know that she had not promoted the abortion, but then I had to forgive my ex-girlfriend for lying to me.

Today my wife and I minister to young people at our church and are spiritual parents to them. It has been a blessing to be godly influences to them.

Having my child's plaque on The Wall at the National Memorial for the Unborn is a statement of truth. A child's life was lost because of sin, a bad decision, and misinformation. It is a warning to those who are thinking of following the same traumatic pathway, and it is a statement of God's forgiveness and grace. Praise God for its presence and His presence with it. God bless you.

—Scott Miller

And God is able to make all grace abound to you, so that in all things at all times, having all that you need, you will abound in every good work.
2 Corinthians 9:8

MICHAEL MAIN
Fall 1985
Psalm 139—Forgive Me, I Love You

"Young girls who get pregnant should be encouraged to have abortions, and my daughter would have one if she got pregnant as a teenager."

Mother's comment replayed through my mind when I learned that at age eighteen I was pregnant. I was alone in a new city. I couldn't tell my parents for they would think I was a failure just as I started college. Neither pregnancy nor being grandparents was in the plans for them or me.

The counselor at the pregnancy center focused on the negatives a baby brings, along with complications a young mother could not handle. In a subtle way, she implied that my life would be ruined. I kept my pregnancy a secret and ultimately ended my baby's life on a Saturday morning at Women's College Hospital in Toronto.

Michael Main was eight-weeks-old in my womb when I made the decision to end his life. His dad, grandparents, aunts, and uncles never knew he existed until years later. My life entered a new phase in which drugs, alcohol, parties, and frequent promiscuity were my focus. Commitment in love and life were a problem for me, so I escaped to a numbing lifestyle that resulted in pain and depression. I tucked the abortion experience deep within me, never to feel the pain of losing my unborn child until nine years later after the birth of my son Matthew.

After falling in love with my husband Jim and my two stepsons Mitchell and Troy, I started to think about the abortion. I looked into the eyes of my five-year-old stepson Troy and thought how Michael would have been exactly the same age. My husband was unaware of my terrible secret, and when I shared it with him, he gave me nothing but support, love, and time.

When our son Matthew was nine months old, I went through a secret depression, which I thought had to do with his weaning from breast-feeding and my return to work. I had difficulty sleeping, I cried a lot, couldn't concentrate, and toyed with the idea of suicide. The thought of never seeing my children grow up and religious reasons kept me from going through with it. I decided to tell my husband and get the help I needed.

When I asked God for forgiveness and talked with Him about my problems, information and helpful people started to surface. I heard on the radio about post-abortion syndrome and the National Memorial for the Unborn. God answered my prayers, and I gave my son Michael over to God and now believe he is fine and loved. I resolved my issues with post-abortion syndrome and put my experience to use with an agency called Birthright, providing people with loving alternatives. I am able to visit with Michael, as I have placed the duplicate plate I was given at a cemetery in my town that honors the unborn. Thank God for places such as the National Memorial for the Unborn, the forgiveness of sins, and the fact that I will hold my Michael in my arms when I am called home, and God will hold me.

"Romance fails us—and so do friendships—but the relationship of mother and child remains indelible and indestructible . . . the strongest bond on earth." (Theodore Reik)

—Debbie Garriock

Can a mother forget the baby at her breast and have no compassion on the child she has borne? Though she may forget, I will not forget you! See, I have engraved you on the palms of my hands.
Isaiah 49:15, 16

TO STEPHANIE AND STEPHEN
We'll Soon Be Together

I was the all-American-girl—blonde hair, blue eyes, and had everything going for me. I was a cheerleader and took lessons in ballet, baton, piano, flute, horseback riding, and even attended charm school. I was given it all, but I lost it when I became pregnant. I knew what would happen if our families found out. My stepfather was an influential attorney in town. The boy I dated was from a wealthy family, attended a private school, and had a promising future in college football. I could not wreck his plans or dreams. So on Valentine's Day, I aborted my child.

After my abortion, I dealt with my pain alone. To my boyfriend the abortion was obviously no big deal. Within three months, we broke up. That summer my parents went to Hawaii and considered me responsible enough to stay home alone. My boyfriend showed up again, and I got pregnant again.

My brother helped me get an abortion because I couldn't bring myself to tell my mother. When she went out of town for two weeks in October, I was nearly twelve weeks pregnant. It was almost too late for a first trimester abortion. The pain was so unbearable that my brother heard me in the waiting room screaming, "Oh, God, it hurts! I want my mother!" While my boyfriend went on with his life, I crawled in a hole.

Years later when I married my husband, neither of us realized the baggage this would bring into our marriage. When I was pregnant with our son Zac, I would plead to the Lord, *Let this baby be healthy and whole. I know I don't deserve it after what I've done.* Since then we've had countless infertility problems—miscarriages, surgeries. I carry the guilt that I might be responsible for my own condition due to the choices I made.

I used to dread going to heaven and worried that the children I aborted would not want to see me. Now I know that my Father God will show me my children, and He will reunite us. It will be wonderful.

—Debbie Johnson

"This is the covenant I will make with the house of Israel after that time," declares the L<small>ORD</small>. *"I will put my law in their minds and write it on their hearts. I will be their God, and they will be my people."*
Jeremiah 31:33

NICOLAS
April 20, 1995
Heaven's Treasure — Gran

On April 20, 1995, my son's girlfriend's mother called me demanding money for her daughter's abortion. Since her daughter was only fifteen, she threatened to have my boy locked up for statutory rape. Our son loved this young girl and was completely torn apart by the devastating circumstances. I told the girl's mother that I would never pay to have my grandchild murdered. She refused to allow me to speak to the girl and insisted that it was her daughter's choice.

After the abortion that evening, my son called to say he would be staying with his girlfriend. He had sold something valuable to pay his half. The fifteen-week old baby was a boy.

My son was soon headed on a collision course with self-destruction. My suffering over this was great, but it was nothing compared to his. We have suffered through these past few years with him, and he seems to think he needs to be punished.

Now my son understands what happened to his baby during the abortion procedure. I am able to share my pain with my best friends and family, but his friends are so young that none of them have ever experienced any trauma. They cannot begin to help him through it.

My two best friends came with me to visit the National Memorial for the Unborn recently. We spent more than an hour reading the names of the babies remembered on The Wall. We cried, prayed, and mourned for those little ones—the pain they suffered in death and for the pain and suffering of those left behind.

    Grandparents are deeply affected by abortions, and their stories need to be told. Abortion does not strike the parents alone, although I'm sure their pain is greater. Our loss as grandparents is no less deeply felt and needs to be expressed, experienced, and put to rest.

—Patty Stewart

Even when I am old and gray, do not forsake me,
O God . . . you who have done great things.
Who, O God, is like you?
Psalm 71:18, 19

OUR PRECIOUS JESSI
July 14, 1993
Jesus Gives Us a Future

When I was sixteen, I became pregnant by my boyfriend. I decided to keep my baby from the start. For weeks, I followed her development with medical books and pictures. I took vitamins, drank juice, and ate vegetables I hated, even when I felt too sick to eat. When I felt scared, I talked to the life inside me. My hand was never far from my stomach. Before anyone knew I was pregnant, it was easy to believe that everything would be all right somehow. But when I finally got the courage to tell others, I had to face their fear, too, and it changed everything.

When I told my baby's father I was pregnant, he quickly offered to help me. I loved him, but I knew he was scared, and he couldn't support a baby. He was dating someone new, and I knew that he cared for her a lot.

When I finally told my parents of my pregnancy, they were devastated. They pleaded with me to have an abortion, but I felt I'd rather die than hurt my baby. When I didn't change my mind, they asked me to leave. My parents are good, caring people, but they were afraid for our family and me. They were dying inside, and their pain affected me even more than my own.

When I realized what my decision to keep the baby involved, I became afraid.

Afraid of what people in church would say when they found out.

Afraid that no man would love me if I had a baby.

Afraid that I could never fulfill my dreams of becoming a doctor.

Most of all, I was afraid of being alone.

In spite of my fears, I wanted to do the right thing. Then well-meaning people told me that God understood my need for an abortion. It was the responsible thing to do. Having a baby at my age would be unfair to so many people, they said.

My parents said my baby wasn't a person yet, and the obstetrician agreed. How could abortion be wrong when so many people accepted it? I let my feelings cloud my judgment, and I closed my heart completely.

Waiting for the abortion was agonizing. I still had morning sickness, and it broke my heart. It reminded me that the life inside me was still growing, even though it was going to have to end. I remember wishing that abortion wasn't legal. People say it gives women a choice, but I felt I didn't have one. Since abortion was available, it was my duty to choose it.

Even before I went to the clinic, I decided I'd never let myself regret it. Some women did, but I vowed to be different. And for a while, I was. After my abortion, I went back to being sixteen, and my family pretended that I'd never been pregnant. For the next couple of years, I worked hard in school and thought success would justify my sacrifice. But I wondered why I felt that way, since I believed I hadn't lost anything. There was a pit inside me that I dared not go near.

Then one day at the movies, I saw it on the big screen: HURTING AFTER AN ABORTION? The girl with the sad eyes in the crisis clinic's ad even had my long dark hair. I memorized the phone number and called that night. The counselor said that every woman who's had an abortion deals with tough feelings eventually. I argued that I didn't regret my decision, that I did *not* have feelings to deal with. But I couldn't say the word *baby* or look at a pregnant women or hold a teddy bear or buy a goldfish or touch my stomach or be reminded that I had a heartbeat. I wish I could explain how *not* normal I was, how empty, while telling the counselor how normal and *not* regretful I was at the same time.

When I read about the National Memorial for the Unborn, I was angry. I thought they wanted to hurt me when I was trying to be strong. They had no right to memorialize the unborn, when I'd earned the legal right to say that my baby wasn't a person.

I don't know why, but I called that counselor again and made an appointment to talk with a woman named Vicki, who'd had an abortion, too. I went there to convince her that abortion was okay so I could convince myself. But as we talked, I started to see what I had really done and why I'd been so afraid to admit it. It had never occurred to me that I would see my baby in heaven if abortion was wrong, and it really was a baby. Somehow I couldn't get past my belief that a baby didn't count until it was fully formed. I thought that if abortion were wrong, I had lost a child God would never resurrect, even if He'd wanted her to be born. I would stop hurting if I could prove that my unborn baby had not been a person. But God healed my scars in a much better way. He used Vicki to give me a hope that I'd never dared to let myself have. I had come to the clinic that day with an indescribable emptiness, but I left with a priceless gift. I know now that I'll hold my baby someday.

I'd like to say that it's been easy since then, but it takes courage to keep this hope alive in a world that values the unborn so little. The National Memorial for the Unborn has given me that courage. Whenever I feel crazy for believing that my tiny unborn baby matters to God, I go to The Memorial to read the plaques, and the faith of the other moms encourages me. Having a plaque for my own baby reminds me that I have a future with a precious child named Jessi. I am in awe of my Savior.

—Anonymous

I pray also that the eyes of your heart may be enlightened in order that you may know the hope to which he has called you, the riches of his glorious inheritance in the saints.
Ephesians 1:18

> **ROBERT FRANCIS LITTLE III**
> January 22, 1976
> *Safe with Jesus*

> **HOPE**
> March 21, 1980
> *Psalm 40:3*

> **FAITH**
> December 30, 1980
> *Luke 7:50*

I have had three abortions. The first occurred when I was married to an abusive husband and already had two small sons. Since I heard that abortion was legal and safer than childbirth, I didn't want to bring another child into a violent environment.

Within one year, I moved 1,400 miles away from that environment. I immediately got involved in another relationship and became pregnant. I believed the father who said abortion was my only option. As a single parent, I would have to quit my job, go on welfare, and complicate the lives of my two young sons. The first abortion left me numb. The subsequent abortions came easily, as I had desensitized myself to all feelings by using drugs.

Seven years after the last abortion, I decided to volunteer at a crisis pregnancy center, not realizing they were Pro-Life. I was shocked when I learned the truth about fetal development and abortion techniques in the training class. I succumbed to deep depression and was on the brink of suicide. Even after going through Bible study for post-abortive women, I couldn't get past it. My Bible study leader led me through an inner healing where I retraced the last thirteen years of my life back to the first abortion. Jesus came and showed me my children in heaven, safe with Him. My heart was healed at that moment, and he later inspired me to write this poem:

I see my son
Wrapped in blue
Safe in Jesus' arms
Whole and new.

What is this gift?
So undeserved
This glimpse into Heaven
When the horror of my sin
Has me so unnerved.

I see his little arms
Waving back and forth
As if to say, "In Heaven,
I am of great worth."

"Don't cry for me,"
They seem to say.
"I love you, Mom;
It's okay."

I see my son now with peace and love
Ever grateful to Jesus
For the precious assurance
Of Heaven above.

—Joan Phillips

For the Lamb at the center of the throne will be their shepherd;
he will lead them to springs of living water. And God
will wipe away every tear from their eyes.
Revelation 7:17

Jesus said to the woman,
"Your faith has saved you; go in peace."
Luke 7:50

He put a new song in my mouth, a hymn of praise to our God.
Many will see and fear and put their trust in the L ORD.
Psalm 40:3

SELAH STEWART
January 5, 1990
Psalm 139:13–16

Although I have never personally had an abortion, our whole family lost a child to abortion. My husband and I have never been able to conceive a child, but God has blessed us with one son and two daughters through the amazing gift of adoption.

The child we lost to abortion, Selah, was the biological sibling of one of our daughters. Some might consider Selah and our daughter as unwanted children, but we know that every child is both planned and wanted. The Creator Himself knits each irreplaceable, precious life together in a mother's womb. Each child should be welcomed as a wonderful gift from His hand.

When we learned that our daughter's birthmother had aborted a child, we mourned for Selah. We truly feel we have lost a member of our family. Our daughter is too young to understand that she has lost a brother or sister. When I look at her, I wonder if Selah resembles her. Our daughter has a beautiful musical quality to her voice, and this influenced me in choosing a name for her sibling when I ordered our plaque. The word "Selah" appears many times in the book of Psalms to indicate a musical rest. Selah's life here was tragically silenced by abortion, but she now rests in heaven, tenderly cradled in the Shepherd's arms. We extended our family name to Selah, also.

The National Memorial for the Unborn is a great comfort to us. It's a tangible place where Selah's memory is honored and which we can visit as we wait for our joyful and heavenly reunion. It has been marvelous to see God take my sorrow and use it for good.

Our loss has served as a catalyst for me to pray for women in a post-abortion Bible study. We do not know if Selah's birthmother has repented of her abortion, but we fervently pray that she will experience Christ's loving mercy, healing, and forgiveness. One day we will stand together with Selah in the joy of God's own presence.

—Elsa Stewart

He tends his flock like a shepherd: He gathers the lambs in his arms and carries them close to his heart; he gently leads those that have young.
Isaiah 40:11

All the days ordained for me were written in your book before one of them came to be.
Psalm 139:16

SETH
January 1978
Son, I miss you

I am a sinner saved by grace. Jesus Christ took all my sin, shame, and guilt on the cross with Him. My sins are forgiven, and He remembers them no more. Isn't that amazing? He did that for me because I accepted His free gift of life and forgiveness.

This is so simple, and yet my Master's degree didn't give me this wisdom. This wisdom comes from the Bible and knowing the Lord Jesus Christ personally. If I had known Jesus could forgive my sin of adultery, I would not have tried to cover it up by having an abortion and moving deeper into the strongholds of Satan.

I blame myself for listening to Satan, the father of lies, and allowing him to prey on my fears. He used other people to tell me lies, such as:

- It isn't a baby, only a mass of cells.
- We don't need more unwanted and poor children in this world.
- You wouldn't make a good mother at your age without a husband.
- You could help the overpopulation by not having this child.
- Don't bring an illegitimate child to us!

- Adoption is not the answer. It will only hurt you, and who knows who the parents might be or what they might do to your child?
- Abortion is the easy way out.

I should not have listened to this unwise counsel that led to the biggest mistake of my life and one made in haste.

The condemnation for my abortion happened every time I saw a baby. How I had loved babies! My childhood had been full of babysitting and preparations to be a good mother, but after the abortion, I couldn't even look at a baby because of my guilt. I had haunting nightmares of murder and being murdered. The abortion tore at every relationship I had until it destroyed it. Can you imagine the loneliness and isolation that fifteen years of destroyed relationships can bring? My constant companions were shame and depression. I became a workaholic and developed stomach problems and headaches. I formed excessive work habits to try to improve my deteriorated self-esteem.

The good news is, the Lord did the impossible. Secular counselors were unable to help or even find the root of my problem, but the Lord healed it all. When I allowed Him to work in my life and love me, He gave me "gladness instead of mourning" (Isaiah 61:3). He has healed my wounds and has set me free from my bondage to Satan. God has also made up for my wasted years "the years the locusts have eaten" (Joel 2:25). The Lord ended my loneliness and gave me a loving and accepting husband who led me to Christ. Now I am His maidservant, and He uses me for the divine purposes for which He created me.

The plaque in memory of Seth at the National Memorial for the Unborn is a tangible item belonging to Seth that I hold dear. It is a statement for all to read that I am a mother who longs for her son, and I know we will be reunited in heaven. Now I go on with my life and love my other sons.

Can you imagine such a loving God? He entrusted me with two more sons even though He knew the wrong I had committed. An earthly father might have held this against me forever and never trusted me with such a precious gift again. Satan wanted me to believe that God would punish me by never allowing me to have another child or by losing a baby after birth. I am thankful God gave me two more children.

God is not a punishing and unforgiving Father. Yes, He allowed me to suffer the consequences of my sin, but when I cried out to Him in my despair, He answered me. Praise the Lord who loves the lost and forgives sinners. He has revealed His loving kindness by healing my deepest wounds and helping me to forgive myself. What an awesome God who can use the ugliest part of my life to accomplish His work and bring healing to others.

—Mary Cowan

Paul, a servant of God and an apostle of Jesus Christ for the faith of God's elect and the knowledge of the truth . . . resting on the hope of eternal life, which God, who does not lie, promised before the beginning of time, and at his appointed season he brought his word to light through the preaching entrusted to me by the command of God our Savior.
Titus 1:1–3

He has sent me . . . to comfort all who mourn, and provide for those who grieve in Zion—to bestow on them a crown of beauty instead of ashes, the oil of gladness instead of mourning, and a garment of praise instead of a spirit of despair.
Isaiah 61:3

> **STACIA GRACE REYNOLDS**
> Summer 1977
> *Until We Meet and Hold Hands*

> **MICAH TIMOTHY REYNOLDS**
> Summer 1978
> *Until We Meet and Hold Hands*

As we crossed a busy street, I told my three sons to hold each other's hands so we would cross safely. I glanced at them, blond and happy in the warmth of the spring afternoon. I felt the familiar tug at my heart as I realized that only part of our family was here with us. Gone were my five other children—two the victims of abortion, the latter three from miscarriages brought on, I'm sure, by my abortion history.

When I was sixteen, I was frightened when I found out I was pregnant. My boyfriend—who is now my husband—was seventeen, and he was scared also. My abortion was traumatic, painful, and incomplete. Twenty-four hours later, I delivered my baby at home, once again alone and frightened. I became pregnant again one year later.

People ask me, "If the first abortion was so bad, why did you get pregnant again?"

I tell them I needed to replace the emptiness in my heart for something I didn't have. Years later, I would find out the clinical name for this second pregnancy was the *atonement baby*. Once again, I aborted.

My husband and I married two years after the second abortion. It would be putting it mildly to say we had a rocky marriage. So many dynamics play into a marriage when a couple creates life and then destroys it. I suffered three miscarriages over the next seven years until I gave birth to my sixth child (my first living child).

I suffered for seventeen years in silence because of the shame and guilt of those abortions. But one night, I met a special man who heard my cries of agony. His name is Jesus Christ, and He changed my life. He assured me that He forgave me but I needed to forgive myself.

In a post-abortion Bible study, I talked openly and honestly with other post-abortive women. I found that we are ordinary women who may sit next to you at church on Sunday. We may be your mom, your sister, the Kool-Aid mom that your children adore. We must not hide anymore, because if we do, how will other woman find healing?

I now volunteer at a crisis pregnancy center and am involved in our post-abortion Bible study. I tell the suffering women that God has plans for them. And one of those plans is that they walk in glory in the sunlight of His love and not in the shadows anymore.

Yes, my precious Stacia Grace and Micah Timothy are safe with Jesus. I have put up plaques in their memory until we meet and hold hands.

—Kathleen Reynolds

I saw the Holy City, the new Jerusalem . . . The city does not need the sun or the moon to shine on it, for the glory of God gives it light, and the Lamb is its lamp.
Revelation 21:2, 23

STEPHANIE CATHERINE
April 1969
You Are Deeply Missed

I was engaged when I became pregnant. My fiancé and I were both college students at Michigan State University. He felt trapped and became physically involved with at least two other coeds. I gave him the diamond ring back. It was over. The baby seemed so unreal. It was referred to as a *pregnancy*. Abstract. No emotion. I was desperate but no one referred me to a counselor, an adoption agency, or anyone who could help me resolve this double-crisis in my life.

The doctor at the campus clinic asked me if I wanted to be pregnant.

"No," I responded.

"Ten minutes, and you won't have to think about it for the rest of your life," was his retort.

He was wrong.

Fourteen years later at my work site, a single coworker became pregnant. I had to interact with her on a daily basis. My defenses and denial crashed. I realized that I could have been the one carrying a baby to term. After work I'd go home, lay down, and cry. Dealing with the grief and loss of what really happened on the abortion table was critical. It was my baby, the child I'd never had.

Today Stephanie Catherine lives in my heart, and I love her dearly.

—Karen K.

When I am afraid, I will trust in you....
Record my lament; list my tears on your scroll—
are they not in your record?
Psalm 56:3, 8

TIFFANY NICOLE BURTON
December 18, 1974
My Only Child

I was raised in a Christian family, and life seemed great for me as I was growing up. Then at age fifteen, I had a relationship with an older man. I thought I was experiencing love, but I found myself in a crisis pregnancy. The father of the baby told me an abortion would solve the "problem." After all, he had helped a former girlfriend get one, and it was okay. He knew much was at stake—my parents and church finding out, and our age. I was confused and thought this was the only way to get myself out of this situation.

On December 18, 1974, the father of my baby picked me up from high school and drove me to the abortion clinic. I have never forgotten that day. Several of us were in a room waiting when I talked with a married woman who also was having an abortion. She explained that it was not the right time in their life for a child. Since she seemed so in control, I felt I had to be strong and not show I was afraid. Then the father drove me back to the school grounds where I was picked up for the ride home. It was a long ride home.

At first, I felt relieved that this was our secret, and no one would ever know. I never realized how hard it would be for me to live with my choice. I began drinking and got involved in drugs. The relationship with this man lasted five years.

Finally, I walked out one night because I could no longer take his emotional abuse.

Then I met my future husband, the man of my dreams, and we married. He was so kind, gentle, and sincere. I had found someone who really loved me and would not hurt me. However, my abortion experience would not go away. I did not want any children at first. I felt I could not be a good mom. After all, look what I had done. I did not want to be reminded and tried not to feel the pain. I continued drinking and using drugs. December 18 was a difficult day for me every year, as well as Mother's Day and any time the subject of abortion came up.

After ten years of marriage, we separated, and I remember crying out to God, *I have ruined everything in my life—my child and my marriage!* There had to be more to life. Because I knew my abortion was wrong, I could not face God so I left the church. But now He was the only one I knew to cry out to. That's when I found Jesus with His arms open wide waiting to take me in. I found it difficult to read in the Bible that God as the Creator knits us together in our mother's womb.

So I gave my life to Christ as Lord and Savior. My ex-husband also gave his life to Christ, and God restored our marriage. He has changed my life forever and has given me the peace and joy I was searching for. I now have a personal relationship with God and am following His path for my life. What freedom and joy I have!

My healing began when I went through a post-abortion Bible study. I allowed Christ to come into that dark place where I had buried the memories of my abortion. He cleansed it with His blood, forgave me, and set me free. He has healed my wounds and mended my broken heart through His grace and mercy.

Placing a plaque at the National Memorial for the Unborn was such an honor for me. My daughter will always have a special place in my heart until I see her one day in heaven. She has a place here where she can be remembered, even though she never made it into the world.

As of this date, I have never conceived another child. So not only did I kill my child, but she was my only child.

—Sue Burton Illig

Thus you will walk in the ways of good men and keep to the paths of the righteous. . . . Trust in the LORD with all your heart and lean not on your own understanding; in all your ways acknowledge him, and he will make your paths straight.
Proverbs 2:20; 3:5, 6

> **TRAVIS ISAIAH KASDORF**
> August 1981 John 15:13
> *In Loving Memory of Our Son*

> **AMBER YAKIRA KASDORF**
> February 1982 2 Samuel 12:23
> *In Loving Memory of Our Daughter*

Ty and I met in eleventh grade while attending a Christian school. We began dating and shortly after engaged in premarital sex. Without considering the consequences of our immature decisions, our sexual intercourse lacked the use of consistent birth control. We thought I would never become pregnant. Unfortunately, our ignorance and lack of self-control led to my pregnancy with a son.

Because I was raised in a Christian home, attended church, and was enrolled at a Christian school, I felt afraid, confused, and overwhelmed. Appearances played a vital role in my family. My parents had warned me to never come home pregnant. Moreover, I feared expulsion from our Christian school. Assuming my parents were unapproachable concerning my pregnancy, I felt like a bear in a trap willing to gnaw off his leg to save himself.

Feeling I had nowhere to go, I turned to Planned Parenthood and ultimately chose abortion. At first, I struggled with the morality of the decision.

"Is it a baby?" I asked.

The counselor gave me all the answers. "No, it's not a baby; it's just cartilage like your ear. It's a blob of tissue."

She never informed me he had a beating heart, legs, arms, hands, and feet.

"Can I have children again?" I asked.

"Oh, yes, you can have children in the future," she assured me.

After my first abortion, Planned Parenthood prescribed the diaphragm. Pregnant again, we made a second decision to abort. This time I felt like a lamb led to the slaughter. I was silent with no emotions, no tears, no questions. I just did it and was done with it. My heart had hardened.

For ten years, I was pro-choice. I justified my actions by feeling anger toward the Pro-Life movement for not supporting pregnant women. But I never asked about their services. After all, it was my body, and I could do what I pleased with it.

Ty and I married in 1983, a year after my second abortion. After seven years of marriage, I became pregnant with my daughter. At the time, I was attending a university, and this made the pregnancy as equally inconvenient as the others. There were two differences. I was married, and Ty wanted to begin a family. When my daughter was twelve weeks old, I watched her movements on the ultrasound screen. I could see her heart beating. Yet my remorse for my abortions never surfaced. After I gave birth to my daughter, I still felt no remorse. However, I had a difficult time bonding with her while she was young. I never realized that this is a symptom of the post-abortion syndrome, resulting from past abortions. Two years passed, and one day while watching my daughter, it finally hit me—I had killed my two children. I wept bitterly. My heart ached to hold my babies. Falling to my knees in prayer, I asked God for His forgiveness for my selfishness and deceit. Thankfully, He picked me up and gave me the courage to go on. Now I long to see my children in the glory of God's presence.

To place a plaque at the National Memorial for the Unborn has had a significant impact on me. It provided a time of healing, of acceptance, and an opportunity to let go of past pain associated with the death of my unborn children, and to honor them respectfully. The Memorial allowed me to acknowledge publicly that my children did exist. They no longer are hidden in the deep, dark secret of abortion. They were more than just cartilage and blobs of tissue. They were tiny living beings created in the image of God.

—Carolyn Kasdorf

Greater love has no one than this, that
he lay down his life for his friends.
John 15:13

But now that he is dead, why should I fast?
Can I bring him back again? I will go to him,
but he will not return to me.
2 Samuel 12:23

WILLIAM ANTHONY
I Loved You and Your Daddy

In 1962, I was nineteen years old and a sophomore in college. I was engaged to the man I adored, expecting to be married in eight months. I got pregnant the first time we made love so we went to Tahoe and were married. After we moved in with his parents, he started dating another girl I knew from school and withdrew from me. The problem was that his parents had always planned for him to compete in the Olympics, and a pregnant wife and subsequent grandchild were not part of the agenda. I felt so betrayed and ostracized by him and his family that after a few months, I asked his mother to put me on a plane for home.

When I arrived, my parents told me his parents claimed I was not carrying his child. They did not offer to support me at all. By now, I was seven months pregnant. I loved the child, and I loved my husband dearly, but I had only two options: look in the phone book for a home for unwed mothers or get an illegal abortion. I told Mother to ask their attorney where I could get an abortion.

The attorney made the arrangements. My father contributed five hundred dollars for the abortion, but he was angry about the money. Mother took me to a street corner where I got into a waiting car. Someone blindfolded me and pushed me down on the floor of the backseat. When we reached our destination, the blindfold was removed and I was led to a bedroom in a small house. A woman told me a rubber tube would be inserted into my uterus to kill the baby in utero. In about ten days, there would be a bad odor. I would have contractions and go through the normal childbirth of a dead baby.

I was fully aware of the risk I was going through. But if this was all right with my husband and parents, then it was all right with me if I died.

A huge black woman came in carrying a glass vial with a rubber tube in it. She had me spread my legs on the bed and inserted the rubber tube into my uterus. I felt as if I were being butchered alive, like a small Easter bunny on my grandmother's kitchen table being chopped in two.

In ten days, I went through about four hours of labor and delivered my fully developed dead baby boy into the toilet. My mother burned him in the incinerator. Even though I hemorrhaged for three weeks, I never received any medical attention because of the illegality issue. The attorney got an annulment for my husband and me on the grounds that there was no consummation. My husband later became an Olympic champion, and after that a gutter drunk.

At age fifty-five, I went through a post-abortion recovery workshop for the abortion I had thirty-six years previously. In my mind, I have properly buried my son and have told him about God and Jesus. I believe my son has forgiven me, and I have forgiven myself. I miss all the fun we could have had together, and all the hugs and kisses. I have never spoken openly about this with my family, but I have forgiven them completely. I reconciled with God many years ago.

—Anonymous

Bear with each other and forgive whatever grievances you may have against one another. Forgive as the Lord forgave you.
Colossians 3:13

BABY

I grew up in the Chattanooga area in a church-going, middle-class family, the youngest of three daughters. I excelled in school and never drank, took drugs, or smoked. Although my parents argued a lot, my good grades seemed to make them happy and bring them together.

At seventeen, I started dating a boy from school. One summer night, we had unprotected sex and my worst nightmare came true. Suddenly, I had a decision that I never thought I would have to make. My mother always told us girls that we had a choice. Since I was going to college with a full scholarship, the choice seemed clear. No one in our family had given birth out of wedlock, and I was not about to be the first. Also, marrying the father was not an option because I didn't love him, and we were not ready. Finally, I didn't want to let my family down, and unlike today, AAA (crisis pregnancy center) did not exist.

The solution I chose for my problem was the beginning of a painful chapter in my life. The abortion itself was more physically and emotionally painful than I had ever imagined. However, when it was over, I felt a brief sense of relief. But as time went by, I had periods of deep depression, and I turned away from God. I blamed him for my pain, and I blamed myself. I tried to fill the hole in my heart with alcohol and men.

As technology advanced, intrauterine cameras showed different stages of fetal development on television. This was not a clump of tissue; this was a child! The pain of guilt seemed unbearable, and I contemplated suicide. Fortunately, I never acted on those feelings.

Outwardly I seemed successful. I graduated from college, got married, and started a business with my husband. Later, I started visiting churches just before we adopted our baby girl. I wanted her brought up right. Two years later, I visited a church where I heard Linda Williams, from AAA Women's Services, give her testimony. I met her afterwards, and she encouraged me to sign up for post-abortion counseling, now called ARISE.

Inside, I desperately wanted healing and peace, but I was nervous and emotional at the first meeting. Before I left the second meeting, our leader asked us what area of our lives had been most affected by the abortion. I wrote down—*My relationship with Christ*. Later that night as I was driving home, the walls around my heart crumbled, and all the emotions I had bottled up burst from me as I cried out, *Father, forgive me!* Immediately, I felt God's peace envelop me.

That night my relationship with Christ moved from my head to my heart. Every time I opened the Bible, it was real to me, not just words on paper. His forgiveness and mercy were there for me! My life radically changed. My marriage was saved, and my husband and I both stopped drinking, even though we had abused alcohol for more than a decade. We are now active members of a church. The ARISE Bible study was a major turning point in my life and the life of my family. The seventeen years that I suffered with this secret are like lost years, but since my salvation and healing, I have found peace and joy only God gives through His Son, Jesus Christ.

—Anonymous

Through Christ . . .

*In whom we [I] have redemption,
the forgiveness of sins.*
Colossians 1:14

*Who shall separate us [me]
from the love of Christ?*
Romans 8:35

*I can do everything through him
who gives me strength.*
Philippians 4:13

ROBERT HWANG
January 1981
Son of Un-Suk and William

In 1980 I was a military officer stationed in California. During *happy hour* at the officer's club one Friday night, I met a woman named Un-Suk (she is no longer known by this name). Although she was married to another officer, she initiated a sexual relationship, and I did not protest. In the beginning, we were secretive about our liaisons, but when her husband was reassigned overseas, she stayed at the base for several more months. I insisted she use birth control, so the base doctor gave her an IUD. I tried to use condoms, but decided I didn't need any. She told me a few times during this period that she loved me, but I never reciprocated with words of love to her. In January 1981, her birthday gift to me was sex. In March she told me she was pregnant.

At first, I was pleasantly surprised, but the reality of the situation quickly set in. I convinced myself that the only alternative was for her to have an abortion. After all, she was married to someone else. I did not want to marry her because we had little in common. Furthermore, I did not want to be saddled with a child at the tender age of twenty-five for I had my whole life ahead of me. She did not want to have an abortion and tried to appeal to a natural desire for a man to have a son. But

I insisted. As the weeks went by and she did not get the abortion, I grew angry. I offered to pay my fair share in what I thought was a magnanimous gesture. Finally in April, she drove herself to a hospital in a large city near the base and had the abortion there. She didn't want the word to get around the base that she had gotten pregnant while her husband was overseas.

When she returned from the hospital, I walked to her house under cover of darkness, wanting to see her. It took several minutes of coaxing for her to even let me in the house. I will never forget what I saw when she let me in. Her face was a mask of grief and horror that I had never seen on a person before. At that moment, I knew abortion was wrong, despite the fact that it had been legitimized by a decision of the Supreme Court. I held her in her bed for hours until she told me she was feeling better. I will never forget the irony of her speaking those words while being held by the one who had been largely responsible for her horror to begin with. In my selfishness, I couldn't wait to get out of there.

I learned later that this was neither her first abortion nor her first affair. Today I can only imagine what damage was done to her soul and her psyche by having gone through that horror multiple times. She was diagnosed with breast cancer not long after this and returned to her husband. Now more than sixteen years later, I have no idea what became of Un-Suk.

I do know what became of my unborn child, however. In 1992, after the last of many illicit sexual relationships, I finally could no longer deny my own wretchedness, and I asked Jesus Christ to save me. I once had a vision of a child that I believe was my son. That showed me that he was not lost in a waste container but was alive, warm, and well cared for.

Since 1982 I have been in counseling many times, mostly because of severe depression. Likely, the repressed memories of the abortion experience added to my depression.

The story of how my plaque got on The Wall at the Memorial started with the membership secretary at our church. In response to the question of whether or not I had any children, I wrote, "One child, never named, lost to abortion in 1981." She stunned me by saying she thought it was wonderful that I had honored my child by putting that on my application. A few months later, she told me she had heard about The Memorial on the *Focus on the Family* radio broadcast. After several months of contemplation, I chose the name Robert Hwang.

In March 1997, I visited The Memorial for the first time. I arrived on a beautiful spring day, and even though my plaque had not yet arrived from the manufacturer, I experienced The Memorial in quiet, reverence, and tears. Yes, The Memorial is a place of sadness, but it is also a place of hope. Behind each of those plaques is at least one heart changed by God. My hope is that someday every single child lost to abortion will be honored at The Memorial.

—William Heim

For all have sinned and fall short of the glory of God, and are justified freely by his grace through the redemption that came by Christ Jesus.
Romans 3:23, 24

> ## ZAZECKIE TWINS—1980
> *I Will Hold You in Heaven*
> *I Love You . . . Daddy*
>

> ## ZAZECKIE CHILD—1991
> *I Will Hold You in Heaven*
> *I Love You . . . Daddy*
>

When I was approximately twenty years old, my girlfriend became pregnant. We went along with the idea that this was not really a human life, and we had our whole lives ahead of us. So she had an abortion. One week later my girlfriend was still bleeding and went back to the doctor. He performed a second abortion because he believed it was a twin. I swore I would never go through that again.

Ten years later, a married woman who I was seeing became pregnant. I knew it was my child, because God had spoken to me while I was jogging, but I did not know the Lord personally at that time.

In February, my girlfriend told me she wanted to have an abortion, and I said she should have the baby. In fact, a friend advised that I should insist that she have the baby.

As I thought about what he said, I started to believe that it was a baby and that it was wrong to have an abortion.

I felt like an angry dog backed into a corner. There seemed to be no hope. I cried out to God, *If you exist, I need you in my life right now!* Suddenly, the sound of wind filled my house, and I didn't know where it was coming from. Terrified and helpless, I went to bed in a fetal position. I saw a transparent cloud moving in my room. John 3:8 states, "The wind blows wherever it pleases. You hear its sound, but you cannot tell where it comes from or where it is going. So it is with everyone born of the Spirit." I went into a deep sleep, and when I woke up I had one thought on my mind—to pay the difference between the price of an abortion at a clinic or at a doctor's office. I was going to give her seven hundred dollars with instructions not to have an abortion. If she decided to have one, she would have to spend three hundred dollars of her own money. On Friday, I called up my girlfriend and informed her of my decision.

That same day I was driving to meet some friends in the afternoon when I noticed that my girlfriend and her husband were in the car next to me. I had never seen the two of them together. I never saw her again, even though she called sometime later to inform me that she did have the abortion.

Now Jesus was the new love in my life, but I did not know Him in a deep way. Later, as I was reading the Bible, it came alive to me. God spoke to me through His Word! I was overwhelmed by His love and my sinfulness. I knew I was in His awesome, holy presence, and He was convicting me of my sins. I was guilty of breaking all His holy commandments. Then I felt a cleansing love from the top of my head to the bottom of my feet and a new clean heart burning inside. I experienced

His agape love, justice, mercy, forgiveness and righteousness while being in His presence. I was now born again.

It has been over ten years since the Messiah has come into my life. He has given me new life and joy in my heart. In addition, He has given me a beautiful wife and two children. He has restored me!

—William Zazeckie

For Christ died for sins once for all, the righteous for the unrighteous, to bring you to God. He was put to death in the body but made alive by the Spirit.
1 Peter 3:18

MARK STEFFEN BECK
May 1975
Psalm 51:14

I am the only daughter of a doctor in Enid, Oklahoma. I was born again in August 1971, when I was sixteen. I love my parents and feel they did the best job they could, but their love seemed conditional. During the last two years of high school, I was angry at God for not giving me a boy to love. I went to college, started drinking, and gave away my virginity while drunk. When I got pregnant at nineteen, the father said he would marry me, but he changed his mind.

When I told my parents about the pregnancy, Dad decided I would have an abortion, even though I wanted to give my baby up for adoption. We told no one about the baby. My mother always obeyed my father, and I was afraid to disobey him, so I agreed to the abortion. Mother and I went to a Houston clinic where Dad said that they had counselors to help me. Mother paid them five hundred dollars in cash and was told to leave me there. The counselor took all the girls (about twenty-five) and taught us about birth control. That was the last I saw of her. I was given a shot of Demerol, and around midnight the doctor came to my room and injected saline into my uterus. The nurse never told me what would happen. Later, I went to the bathroom and saw my baby hanging from the umbilical cord. As I screamed hysterically for help, I heard the nurses out in the hall talking and laughing. After fifteen minutes, my roommate went to get a nurse. She made me get back in bed with the baby hanging between my legs and said they had to wait until I passed the placenta. I lay in bed crying, trying not to touch the baby with my legs. Finally, they removed it. We went home to Enid, and I had some complications afterwards.

At the clinic I had worn new house shoes my mother had given me. I dripped blood on them when I walked from the bathroom to bed, and I thought Mom would be angry at me because they were expensive. So I wrapped them in a towel and hid them under dresses in the back of my closet when I got home. For several years I took them with me every time I moved to dorm rooms or apartments until I finally realized I could throw them away.

During college I started taking speed, stopped eating, and was anorexic (ninety pounds). I was on antidepressants for twenty years until recently. When I got married, my husband and I tried to have a baby, but we couldn't conceive. I was sure that God was punishing me. Finally we did, and now I have four children. I spent eight years after the abortion in destructive behaviors, going to three different secular counselors and never talking about the abortion. A Christian counselor at Birth Choice helped me examine how I felt about my child, and I grieved for three days and nights. She suggested The Memorial as a place to honor my child, and that has given me peace. I am so glad that my baby isn't forgotten by this world.

I want you to use my real name and not disguise or hide any details. It's time for the world to know the truth of abortion and what it does to women.

—Cindy Hendrickson

Save me from bloodguilt, O God, the God who saves me, and my tongue will sing of your righteousness.
Psalm 51:14

CHRISTOPHER J. BEGEY
1971
You Brought Me to Christ

MARY ANNE STANLEY
1980
You Brought Me to Christ

When my father had a nervous breakdown, I couldn't continue my sophomore year of college. I started hanging around with older men who did drugs and drank. I did not want to live at home and was angry with college, so I just ran off and got married. A few weeks later, my period was late, and I was scared. I had made a mistake about marriage, and I didn't want to tell my mother she was right. I went to a gynecologist and told him I wished I would get my period again. I was nineteen, and didn't know anything about abortion. It was still illegal. Before I knew what had happened, the doctor got a needle out and was yelling at me, and it was over with before he had even explained what he had done.

I started drinking more heavily and became depressed. My marriage went downhill. My husband thought I was still pregnant, and it was a nightmare. He tried to get me involved in wife swapping. I took a year off of college because we couldn't afford to go to school. When I went back to school and lived in the dorm, I got divorced. I started counseling but it didn't last. I would just cry and cry and not know what was wrong with me. After I graduated from college, I moved to Vermont with a new boyfriend. When that didn't work out, I was promiscuous and got pregnant again. This was six years later, and I had no idea how the first abortion had affected me. In the middle of this abortion, I thought about stopping the doctor, but I didn't. This was the swinging sixties and the progressive seventies.

Life continued further downhill, and I became a prostitute. At first it was just stripping in clubs, but it progressed. I got arrested and spent a night in jail. After two years of this, God broke through to me. I became a Christian by the grace of God. I now realize that abortion was a sin and murder. When I was in training to become a sidewalk counselor at Lifeline Ministries, they showed a movie that accurately shows what happens to a baby during abortion. This helped me to move toward healing.

I recently found out about The Memorial, and it was such a blessing. I named my children and wrote on the plaques that they had brought me to Christ. When I found out they are in heaven, I realized God's awesome mercy and love for them and me. The plaques have helped free me from guilt and shame. Thank you, Lord.

—Mary E. Stanley

You adulterous people, don't you know that friendship with the world is hatred toward God? . . . But he gives us more grace. That is why Scripture says: "God opposes the proud but gives grace to the humble." . . . Come near to God and he will come near to you.
James 4:4, 6, 8

JEREMY
May 1970
Jehova (H?) Will Lift Up

I was twenty years old, unmarried, and living with my boyfriend when we found out I was pregnant. He told me to get an abortion. I never questioned him and had it done at eight weeks.

Over the next twenty or more years I denied the fact that I'd committed murder. Initially, I became rebellious toward the baby's father. We married only to separate in less than a year. I got involved in a New Age cult for twelve years. When I began to realize the baby was a person, not a clump of tissue, I was horrified.

In 1985, I became a Christian and started the cleansing process. About four years later, I went through PACE and found God's forgiveness. The memorial service helped me find forgiveness for myself and go on with my life. Now I have the hope of being reunited with my child. The placing of Jeremy's plaque at The Memorial is a testimony to the world that his life changed mine.

—Christine Fischer

> *Be kind and compassionate to one another, forgiving each other, just as in Christ God forgave you . . . For you were once darkness, but now you are light in the Lord. Live as children of light.*
> Ephesians 4:32; 5:8

CORY OWEN-SHELDON
May 1982
Isaiah 40:11a

When I was eighteen years old and in my first semester of college, I became pregnant. I not only was scared myself, but I feared my parents would find out. Although I knew they would want me to have an abortion, I was more concerned that I had disappointed them. My boyfriend told me that if I would have an abortion, we'd only be hurting one person, but if we had the baby, our parents would be shamed.

Ironically, if my boyfriend's parents had known, they would have been adamant about not having an abortion. Once the decision was made, I wanted it over as quickly as possible. When I called the local abortion (family planning) clinic, the man on the phone told me it was urgent that I make reservations right away because the appointments always filled up quickly. He offered no counseling, no alternatives, and no mention of risks. Just urgency!

On that fall afternoon in 1981, I arrived for my appointment. Since general anesthesia was more expensive, I was awake for the whole thing. I remember asking the doctor if it was a boy or a girl, and he said it was too soon to tell. He acted as if this was no big deal. In the recovery room, a girl who had been in a couple of months before commented that they had new snacks this time. I felt as if I was in the middle of a nightmare.

Since I didn't want my family or friends to know what had happened, I went to work that night. I had a physical job that required lifting. Nobody cared, but I couldn't tell anybody what I had just been through.

Afterwards, my boyfriend and I had problems. I blamed him for not talking me out of the abortion. My standards radically changed after that experience. I used drugs and was promiscuous. For three years, I lived with extensive guilt.

When I first came to know the Lord, the biggest obstacle was accepting His forgiveness. Eventually, I backslid but had to accept the truth that I was forgiven and could go forward.

Not a day goes by that I don't think of Cory and how old he would be now. I've become a firm believer in abstinence. The lies they tell you in school health classes led me to believe it was safe to have sex.

A difficult thought occurred to me when I hit my thirties. I not only ended my child's life, but all the children—my grandchildren—that my child would have had.

The Memorial has provided me with a way to let my baby know that he did exist for me, and he was not just a blob of tissue as I once thought. I look forward to seeing him in eternity.

—Stacey B.

Then Jesus said to her, "Your sins are forgiven."
Luke 7:48

He tends his flock like a shepherd:
He gathers the lambs in his arms.
Isaiah 40:11a

> **MICHAEL BUTLER SHAFFER**
> May 19, 1980
> *We're Anxious to Join You in Heaven*

I was in my early twenties when I discovered I was pregnant for the first time. I grew up hearing in my church that abortion murders a human life. So I couldn't face my family, church, and friends with an out-of-wedlock pregnancy. When I told the baby's father about the pregnancy, he left the choice up to me whether I stayed pregnant or had an abortion. He said he would support me either way.

I chose to abort. I was not ready to be a mom. The father and I didn't get along well enough to get married, and I couldn't raise a child alone. I had all the classic excuses to validate my choice.

When I decided to abort, I sank into a deep depression. I begged God to forgive me both before and after the abortion. I tried suicide three times. Obviously, it was not God's will for me to leave this world that soon. He had plans for me. He has used this horrible experience for His glory. I went through post-abortion counseling twice and have had opportunities to speak at churches, at a banquet, and even on local secular TV.

Having placed a plaque at The Memorial has given my son Michael the honor, respect, and closure that he rightfully deserves. On the day I placed his plaque on The Wall, I sensed there was a great celebration in heaven for Michael.

The National Memorial is a place of healing for women and their families who have been through abortion. I found it a place of restoration.

—Pam Shaffer

For God did not appoint us to suffer wrath but to receive salvation through our Lord Jesus Christ. He died for us so that, whether we are awake or asleep, we may live together with him.
1 Thessalonians 5:9, 10

BABY RENARD
July 1980
A Great Loss and Regret

I was sexually active from the time I was thirteen, and I always used birth control pills. But for some reason I stopped using them and used foam instead. I always told myself that if I ever got pregnant, I would just take care of it.

Since I came from a broken home, I never wanted to get married or have children. In fact, I could never accept the fact that children were a result of what I was doing because it was fun. And the medical profession and the world tricks you into believing that a baby is "just a fetus."

In 1980, I returned to college after a three-year break. My girlfriend and my sister had both had abortions, so then when I knew I was pregnant, I sought their counsel. I went immediately for the abortion. The doctor told me it might be too early, and I might have to come back another day. I sat in that waiting room dreading the procedure. I had already spent nights rubbing my abdomen and wondering. I had some young nephews and a niece at the time, and the sight of them made me weak.

The effects of the abortion were mostly emotional. I lashed out at men and only dated unattractive ones. This experience broke me spiritually. When a Jehovah's Witness came to my door one day and asked me if I believed in hell, I told him I had just lived through hell. That conversation started me thinking about and seeking God's forgiveness.

Now I am married with two little boys, ten and eight. Their births were glorious but they were sad reminders of what could have been. Every March I calculate how old my daughter would be now and wonder what she would be like had I given her life instead of taking it away.

Placing a plaque at The Memorial has helped me close that chapter in my life by admitting that I was pregnant and that I did the wrong thing. This whole experience showed me my need for God, and I can now stand delivered, healed, and saved.

—Denise Perehinec

For he has rescued us from the dominion of darkness and brought us into the kingdom of the Son he loves, in whom we have redemption, the forgiveness of sins.
Colossians 1:13, 14

SHANCEY IRWIN
March 3, 1992
With All Our Love—Mom and Dad

I was raised in a Christian home, went to church regularly, and was baptized at the age of thirteen. In addition, I taught Sunday school, worked with the youth while I was in college, and even went on mission trips to Costa Rica. I had a good knowledge of who Jesus was, what He offered, and why I believed in Him. When I was eighteen, my girlfriend conceived a child out of wedlock and decided to abort the baby. We went to Asheville, North Carolina, for the abortion.

After six months of denial and anguish, I finally fell down on my face weeping. Then I felt Jesus saying to me, *I forgive you, even for this I forgive you.* I was somewhat relieved, but I didn't feel I was good enough to do anything for the Lord. So I quit teaching Sunday school, quit working with the youth, quit praying, and quit reading the Bible. I felt I was not worthy of God's forgiveness and therefore not willing to accept it.

Ten years later, my girlfriend Shirley and I got married and had a girl and a boy. I graduated from school and got a job in Chattanooga. Everything was fine and I thought that God was not going to punish us for the great sin we had committed after all. But then I started losing sleep and wondered if I was really saved.

Shirley asked me, "Do you pray and read your Bible?"

"No," I answered.

I could tell this disappointed her, but I could not face my sin. I could not stand to hear the word *abortion*, and I could not even talk to Shirley about it.

Finally, Shirley said, "Why don't you go to the next Bible study you see listed in the church bulletin?"

I agreed, and the next one that came up was for Operation Timothy. I went the first night, and the teacher drew a diagram on the board that described where I was and where I wanted to go, but I did not know how to get there.

A few months later, our assignment was to write our personal testimonies and present them to the class. My turn was coming up, and I had the perfect testimony written out. One evening as I was driving home from work, the Lord seemed to indicate that I should talk about the abortion. I was scared to death but could not resist the Holy Spirit's urging. I hurried home and immediately began writing. That Sunday the group was so supportive as I talked, and a burden was lifted off me.

Frank Peretti in his book, *This Present Darkness,* describes the freedom from torment and the immediate changes in people's lives after their conversion. After I had confessed my sin, the devil could not hold it against me anymore. The Bible study showed me the importance of daily prayer and meditation, one-on-one relationships, and accountability groups. I have a fresh, new yearning to learn more about Christ and to grow closer to Him in my walk.

Now I want to share my experience with everyone. I learned of my spiritual gifts and am trying to glorify God by using them to build His kingdom. Jesus Christ is Lord of my life. He reached down from heaven and saved a wretch like me. I do not forget what I have done and where I have come from. It humbles me when I get proud. It reminds me of His awesome grace, and it helps me understand the wrong things people do.

Now I see that Jesus was with me all along. He was in the waiting room at the abortion clinic, He was there when I was on the floor in my room, He was there when I gave my testimony for the first time, smiling and holding me. Praise be to God.

—Lance Irwin

When you were dead in your sins, . . .
God made you alive with Christ.
Colossians 2:13

LOST GIFT FROM GOD
February 1985
Forgive Me, My Precious Child

The son I will never have is named Caleb. I thought he was just the third child my husband and I weren't going to have when we decided to limit our family to two children. I frequently joked with my friends about Caleb. They just smiled and laughed with knowing looks. I seemed to be getting *baby hungry* again. Then one night, I realized who Caleb was and is. Caleb is the son I will never have because I chose abortion twelve years ago in February of 1985.

I was pregnant right after my eighteenth birthday, when I was a senior in high school. I had been dating the same person for about four years and, obviously, we had an intimate relationship. I can only describe myself as living a double life.

I was one of the top scholars in my school and had finished my first year as a member of the U.S. Army Reserve. By all outward accounts, I was a bright, rising star. But for all my academic knowledge, discipline, and sound judgment, this other lifestyle was going on, too. The man I was dating was five years older than me, though I can't blame him for anything. I wasn't a stranger to the world when I met him. I became sexually active at about thirteen and got involved with alcohol and marijuana in junior high school. We almost married many times over the years until we finally split up for good in my second year of college. In fact, our ill-fated relationship lasted as long as many marriages, so why did we opt for abortion?

When I found out I was pregnant, I shouldn't have been surprised. I had gone to Planned Parenthood several times to get birth-control pills, but I was always afraid to go inside, fearing my parents would find out. I knew girls who had gotten pregnant and had abortions. When I thought I was pregnant, I went to them and found out the details about the clinic in Salt Lake City. I knew about other alternatives, but all of them carried the same consequences: facing my parents and his parents, facing counselors at school who had invested so much in me, and facing my military unit.

I understood that being an unwed pregnant female would result in a dishonorable discharge, and my dreams would end. I didn't want to go through the pregnancy itself because I didn't believe there were that many people who wanted to adopt. I selfishly couldn't give my child away but could justify this "safe, common, and effective procedure."

So there I was, eighteen and pregnant with a bright future but hiding a dark lifestyle. My boyfriend and I debated and talked and cried. Finally, we agreed to go through with the abortion. On the day we drove to Salt Lake City in late February, it was cold and gloomy. I was required to go to a counseling session and review information beforehand and then come back four hours later for the procedure. I remember driving around Salt Lake for hours, waiting with that terrible heaviness in my stomach, hardly talking. *Let it be over soon. I just want to get back to my life*, I thought. I can't really remember what the staff told me at the clinic. I'm sure I wasn't listening; it was so surreal. I do remember looking at pictures and being told how it worked and that most women don't experience any side effects, either physical or emotional.

After a long time, I was called back into the room. The doctor confirmed the pregnancy and performed the abortion. I felt as if my insides were being sucked out of me. The nurse told me several things to watch for and sent me back to the recovery room. After another long wait, I told the nurse I wasn't bleeding, and they took me back in. They explained that not all of the "tissue" had been removed, and they would have to do it again.

I lost my cool and began to cry and say, "No, no, not again!"

The doctor gruffly told the nurse to calm me down while he went to work a second time.

"Are you afraid? Are you in pain?" she asked.

"Yes," I responded. It was then that I caught a glimpse of the blood-covered tool and the sack that held its contents.

I asked for my boyfriend, and they got him. I was overwhelmed. I heard another girl screaming and faintly remember the doctor telling her to shut up. The nurse gave me instructions, papers, and prescriptions for pain. We got in the car and drove back in silence. My boyfriend dropped me off at the park, and I walked home so no one would know I had skipped school to do this.

That night I tried to sleep but didn't rest. My dreams were full of agitation. In the middle of the night, I sneaked out of my house and ran. *Don't do anything physical for a few days until the risk of hemorrhage is past,* echoed the nurse's voice in my mind. I didn't care. I couldn't hold the emotional explosion inside of me that I wasn't supposed to be having. I arrived at my boyfriend's, sneaked up to his room, and woke him up. We both cried. I told him I thought we had done the wrong thing, and he agreed. I asked him why he didn't say so before. He said he was afraid I would be mad since I was the one who had to carry the baby.

The baby—not a procedure or tissue or trash—the baby, our baby.

Neither of us had the courage to do what we knew was right. All we could do was cry and realize the awful truth.

I skipped school for the next month. All those things I wanted to protect were meaningless to me. I got my first "C" grade. I sank into deep depression, and everyone thought I was disappointed over academic competitions I had lost. My life unraveled for about three months. Then I decided to go on and pushed that event down deep into my soul, vowing never to forget it.

Strangely enough, my lifestyle didn't change. But like an avalanche crashing down the mountain is powerless to stop itself, so I was unable to control the deep-seated emotional factors that drove my behavior. I married, became pregnant, and found myself fulfilling all my fears. That child's birth was the reopening of the hidden secret, and I grieved at the awesome knowledge of what had happened that day. But I forced it down again. My life unraveled, and my marriage disintegrated.

I turned to the Lord, and that is the real miracle. He is the only power that can stop avalanches in progress and heal lives out of control. He alone is the most powerful part of my story.

Later, I met and married a wonderful man who showed me how twisted my thinking was about marriage and motherhood, and I had a second child, a son this time. This experience was so different and healing that I even considered having another. I always thought I would call my aborted baby Caleb because the biblical character had such courage and obeyed God. After my second child's birth, I saw an advertisement about the National Memorial for the Unborn and felt compelled to act. I knew I had never dealt with the abortion; I had just suppressed it. I sent for a packet about The Memorial and placing a plaque. I was so relieved to know God could forgive me and that I was but one of countless others. I let the shame and guilt go, but the grief will take time. Now I am able to speak openly about it because I want others to know. A special woman in our church courageously opened up about her experiences, and she works at a crisis pregnancy center doing post-abortion counseling. Her boldness helped me, and I pray that my story will help someone else. Now I know who Caleb is and why the name appealed to me. I am like Rachel weeping for her children: my name is a derivative of hers. Likewise, I have been blessed with two awesome children and a husband who loves us. Thank you, God, for your forgiveness, grace, and mercy.

My hope and prayer is that my children will never have to decide whether to choose between life and death, but if they do, may my experience be a bridge they can walk across in courage and hope. I dedicate this to Aubrey, Michael, and to Caleb, the son I will never have.

—Shelley Goodell

Blessed is he whose transgressions are forgiven, whose sins are covered. Blessed is the man whose sin the LORD *does not count against him and in whose spirit is no deceit.*
Psalm 32:1, 2

BABY SWAFFORD
June 1981
We Loved You Too Late

After college graduation and seven years of marriage, my husband and I were becoming established. He had a good job, I was teaching, and we were in our first home. Things were going well for us, and life seemed complete. We were doing so well on our own that we weren't aware of leaving God out of our lives.

While vacationing at the beach, I discovered that I was pregnant. My husband and I talked it over and decided we weren't ready for parenthood. Our solution seemed simple and uncomplicated: I would have an abortion.

Two friends, one of whom had had five abortions, offered to go out of state with me for the abortion. How I wish they had talked me out of the mistake I was preparing to make. Little wonder that I was desensitized to the clinic's surroundings or to our decision and its ramifications. I was thinking of the freedom I would have to continue teaching and to get my tenured status. My friends and I celebrated my return to *normal life* by dining at a choice restaurant.

But life wasn't normal for a long time thereafter. Women react differently to abortions. Mine hurled me into turmoil. I was deeply troubled without understanding the reason. I took on two more jobs to keep busy and tried to escape by driving over 24,000 miles that year. Still haunted, I shopped, exhausting my credit-card limit and myself. Secretly, I applied for bank loans to cover my debts, solutions that were foreign to me. Somehow, repairing toys filled a need without my realizing that my life needed repairing. That activity became so important that I even resorted to stealing small repair parts. I was at an all-time low, frazzled and in knots from my deceit and lies. I couldn't continue life as it was.

God provided a wise friend who directed me to a Christian counselor and she helped me unravel the tangle of my life. She was patient, kind, and firm, but my recovery took a long time. My husband kindly accepted responsibility for my debts.

God was merciful and led me to a post-abortion recovery group. Their training was the culmination of my recovery. For me, the most effective technique was writing a letter to my unborn child. This promoted healing by helping me sort through my thoughts and understand my reactions. I wanted to help others through the maze of adjustment as I had been helped, so I became a group facilitator. Still later, I led a group in my home.

The National Memorial for the Unborn held a memorial service for our babies. I experienced an emotional release as I confessed my sins and sought forgiveness from God and our unborn child. His will governed my life once more. Through Him, I again realized real freedom as I returned to a healthier, more normal life.

I have given my testimony many times, assured of God's love and forgiveness. God not only gave me peace, but He gave my husband and me the gift of three more children.

My abortion was a life-changing way of learning that a life lived without Jesus Christ at the center would never be complete, happy, or balanced. For me it was a lesson that plunged me from the heights to the depths, but it was a worthwhile lesson considering the outcome. To God be the glory! To God be the glory!

After almost twenty years of teaching, God opened a new door in my career. I am now the office manager for the National Memorial for the Unborn—a place where my final healing came with the placement of our plaque and the memorial service to honor our baby who is waiting for us in heaven.

—Anne Swafford

I have made you and I will carry you;
I will sustain you and I will rescue you.
Isaiah 46:4

TO MY LOST BABY
November 1980
Forgive Me My Trespass

I had never done much dating. When I got to Duke University, I was intimidated by the other girls who were so sophisticated about boys. My single mom, who was disabled and not very involved in my life, raised me. Dad was not a part of my life from the fifth grade on, and I attended a girls' high school. I was a good student and a good girl, but I was headed for trouble.

When a boy asked me out at the beginning of my sophomore year, I was flattered. Within one short month, I was pregnant. We never considered any alternative to abortion. At that time, 1980, abortion was common. Ironically, I felt very cared for by my boyfriend, because he arranged for everything and even agreed to pay half.

When I had my abortion in a doctor's office, the waiting room was full of expectant mothers that morning, most of whom seemed excited to be there. I shall never forget the sounds of the suction machine, the odors of the medical room, or the harsh demeanor of the nurse. I cried uncontrollably for a day. I was very sad at the time, but I quickly buried it.

I got right back to the business of my schoolwork and my various part-time jobs. When I went home for Thanksgiving break I told no one. Within several months, I was getting such poor grades in school that a professor told me, "Frankly, I don't know how you got admitted to this university."

My slide lasted several years, despite the fact that my grades improved. After my undergraduate work, I earned a Master's degree, but my self-esteem was so poor that I spent three years dating a guy who was addicted to drugs.

To earn money to pay my tuition, I worked every Saturday and Wednesday at the local abortion center. The money was great, and I knew what to tell the girls to expect. I passed out birth-control pills, explained what would happen, and even held their hands during the procedure. The sights and sounds were very familiar to me. Once the doctor asked if I wanted to watch the procedure, which I thought would be interesting. Perhaps that was God's way of getting my attention. It was so unforgettable, gruesome, and shocking that I could no longer keep my pain buried.

Meeting and marrying my husband was the beginning of my healing. I was so sure that God would punish me for my abortion by not letting us have children that I was impatient to start our family. My first pregnancy was spent awake at night in tears, sobbing over the lost baby, over my own sin, and over the agony my aborted child endured.

In God's pure grace, He brought a friend into our lives that invited my husband to help establish the National Memorial for the Unborn. My true healing began. Not long afterwards, I enrolled in the PACE Bible study and placed my own plaque at The Memorial. I named my aborted child Grace. I am constantly surprised that good things could come from her death and that, through God's grace, I am a believer. I know I will see her in heaven.

—Ann Caldwell

*For you created my inmost being; you
knit me together in my mother's womb.*
Psalm 139:13

DANIEL
November 13, 1987
Redeemed

I was born into a Christian family. We attended church every Sunday, and my mother was active in all facets of church life—teaching, missions, ministry. My father was a successful businessman. When I was ten, my parents divorced, and my mother, sister, and I moved in with my grandmother. She was a godly prayer warrior. Many times she knelt with me by her bed to pray for our basic needs, and God always provided. I had accepted Christ as a six-year-old child and believed all the Bible said, especially this verse: "Be perfect, therefore, as your heavenly Father is perfect," Matthew 5:48. I needed to be perfect to make up for everything. Like the Pharisees, I wanted my cup spotless on the outside because the inside was so bad. I became judgmental of others who weren't so perfect. The inside of my cup needed some cleansing, though.

Over the years, my cup looked good, but I found it more difficult to keep a personal relationship with my heavenly Father and trust Him to provide. I didn't understand that He wanted me to give Him all the shame, guilt, and hurt I'd been hoarding in secret and to leave it with Him.

After I went to medical school, I felt as if God had abandoned me. I was exhausted, overwhelmed, unhappy, and accused Him of not meeting my needs. In fact, He had—just not in the style to which I wanted to be accustomed! I soon turned to a progressively more sinful and immoral lifestyle that culminated in an unplanned pregnancy. Without hesitation, I terminated the pregnancy with an elective abortion. I couldn't bear any more shame. What I didn't know ahead of time was that there would be two victims that day. Despite incredible pain and suffering, my child would go straight to Jesus, but I would be left behind to grieve. I seemed trapped in a nightmare of sin, pain, guilt, shame, and grief that lasted for years.

After a lifetime as a Pharisee, I could not forgive myself or believe that God could forgive me for that horrible crime. I didn't understand that God had been there in the clinic, watching while His heart broke. He was watching from Calvary while He poured out His life for that sin.

Nothing I did lessened my pain or my guilt. I could never redeem myself. Amazingly, I didn't have to. Jesus already had redeemed me at Calvary all those centuries before. It only took me a second to convince the Father to forgive me, but it took Him years to convince me to receive His forgiveness.

What a mess I'd made of things. I had no future and no hope, but now we get to the good part. When we come to the end of ourselves, God does his best work.

God brought me to Tupelo, gave me a farm, and sent me a husband. In His infinite wisdom, God gave me a man who had an unplanned pregnancy and chose life. His daughter lives because of that choice. Titus 3:4 and 5 says, "When the kindness and love of God our Savior appeared, he saved us, not because of righteous things we had done, but because of his mercy."

C. H. Spurgeon said, "Most of the grand truths of God have to be burned into us with the hot iron of affliction, otherwise we shall not truly receive them."

I, too, learned firsthand that the price of disobedience is high. I've also learned that Jesus paid a high price for that disobedience—His own precious, priceless blood. Because of that, Christ has brought forgiveness, restoration, and peace to this former Pharisee.

I still want to be perfect, and I'm not, but I'm more concerned now about the inside of my cup. There still is plenty in my life and heart for God to work on, and He is working —as I submit to Him. I have spoke frequently in the last two years, telling what God has done in the life of a former Pharisee. You see, we're saved to serve. When I speak, I carry a small block of marble that bears a plaque that says:

DANIEL

November 13, 1987

Redeemed

It is my rock of remembrance. Abortion ended a life, not a lump of tissue. It was the life of my son Daniel. The plaque is a duplicate of one mounted at the National Memorial for the Unborn in Chattanooga, Tennessee, where my son and hundreds of others are memorialized. The names listed there represent only a fraction of the millions of children aborted in this country since 1973. Each name also represents the forty million women whose hearts have been broken by abortion's devastation and the loss of their unborn children.

The block of marble I carry represents not only my broken heart but the healing the Great Physician has so graciously given. As I speak about what God has done, I often pass the marker through the audience. People hold that piece of cold marble in their hands, trace the name and date of Daniel's death, and Daniel becomes real to them. My son was denied life because of my selfishness, but he did not die in vain. Through that small piece of stone, he still speaks.

—Anonymous

See, I lay a stone in Zion, a chosen and precious cornerstone, and the one who trusts in him will never be put to shame.
1 Peter 2:6

DAVID BLAKE
March 15, 1977
Isaiah 54:13

Growing up in a Christian family, I accepted Christ at my mother's knee when I was five years old. As a high school senior, I dated a man in order to feel loved and accepted. Then wine, an empty house, and my naiveté left me wondering what had happened to my virginity. I tried to cover the guilt and growing emptiness by clinging to the relationship with my boyfriend. But I felt incredibly hollow.

I decided that college would fill the void. I entered a university as an honor student, zealously throwing myself into studies. So when I missed my second period in a row, denial set in. I could not even fathom the possibility of being pregnant. I just felt numb.

I vaguely remember going for a pregnancy test. Abortion seemed to be my only choice. It would solve everything. So I called a clinic for information and asked the lady, "Is *it* a baby?"

"No, honey, it's just tissue. After all, you want to finish school, don't you?"

I clung to that statement like a drowning person clutching a life preserver, repeating it over and over until I almost believed it. But deep in my heart I knew the truth that it was a baby, my baby.

I was twenty weeks pregnant—the last week the hospital would do an abortion—and I was too far along for a suction abortion and would have to have a saline procedure. As I drove to the hospital, I uttered an anguished prayer that they would not have room for me. But they had just had a cancellation. I asked again if it was a baby and was firmly told no. By tomorrow it would be all over. As I was led to my room, I felt as if this were only a dream or a movie I was watching. This couldn't happen to me. The familiar numbness wrapped itself around my mind.

Then the needle entered my womb, injecting the deadly salt. Suddenly, I felt my baby recoil. As horror washed over me, I became frantic. The nurses quickly sedated me. I remember little of that long night when my baby died or of his birth the next day. When I struggled to sit up to see my son, the nurses held me down.

They did not tell me that at twenty weeks my baby was fully formed with perfect fingers and unique fingerprints. They did not tell me he was waking and sleeping, sucking his thumb. They did not tell me he could already hear my voice. They did not tell me that he could feel and react to pain.

They did tell me that my life would get back to normal in a couple of days. I returned to school even more determined to find fulfillment in my classes. But a huge, bleeding hole was in my soul. My dreams became nightmares of searching for my crying baby. I added an almost full-time job to my studies so I would be too busy to think or feel.

As my self-esteem hit rock bottom over the next months, I turned to alcohol, drugs, and sex for comfort. Instinctively, I wanted both to punish myself and to stop the pain. I quit school and severed ties with my family. My situation deteriorated, but somehow God reached through my personal fog one night, making me aware of His love. I really didn't think He would want me back after the mess I'd made, but I surrendered to Him in the middle of a party. As God began to remove my coat of numbness, I became painfully aware that I was wearing the dress of guilt. My sleep was still haunted. Hearing a baby cry would tear the wound open once more.

One night as I poured out my heart to God in tearful confession again, He spoke to my heart so clearly that I could almost hear Him audibly. Suddenly, I saw that by refusing to accept His forgiveness, I was saying my standards were higher than God's, and Jesus' death wasn't good enough to pay for my sin. How dare I not accept the gift that Jesus bought with his own blood? I could—yes, I must accept God's forgiveness.

Tenderly, one step at a time, God helped me to experience His forgiveness. My parents found out that I had aborted their first grandchild, which led to a precious time of asking and receiving their forgiveness.

Twelve years after my abortion, a friend introduced me to a post-abortion Bible study. In this small group study, I realized something else was necessary for my complete healing. In addition to dealing with guilt, I had to grieve for my child. I named my son David and found new freedom and peace. Heaven became real for me because I know that my son is waiting there for our reunion.

God began to use my past pain to help others. As director of a pregnancy center, I saw His mighty power firsthand. He miraculously closed down the abortion clinic across the street, then transformed that place of death for over 35,000 babies into a place of life and healing—the National Memorial for the Unborn.

I became a founder of The Memorial. I watched the old dark walls fall under the bulldozer, and light fall on sacred ground stained with so much blood. I helped design The Memorial and have seen God answer our prayers as thousands have found the God who can turn death into life.

I knew my own healing was complete one bright January morning as we dedicated the new Wall of Names amidst tears of sorrow and joy. My parents helped me place a plaque for my son David. Praise to the God who can even use death to give life.

—Linda Keener Thomas

All your sons will be taught by the L*ORD*,
and great will be your children's peace.
Isaiah 54:13

DAVID MATTHEW
November 5, 1982
Genesis 31:49

Fifteen years ago, I was in graduate school and working full-time sixty hours a week. When I started a serious relationship with a fellow student, I wasn't worried about becoming pregnant because my doctor had told me I would have trouble conceiving. As we began a more active sex life, I went to the doctor to get a diaphragm just in case, but it was too late. I was in complete shock with this news, and my boyfriend volunteered to pay for an abortion. He insisted it was the only choice. We could have kids after we got married. I tried to talk him out of the decision, but because of fear and denial, I was easily persuaded. I willingly relinquished control to my boyfriend, my doctor, and my depression. I had a professional career and didn't want to be embarrassed at the office by an illegitimate pregnancy. Having been raised a Roman Catholic, I couldn't confront my family with the shame. Abortion was legal, and that helped me to rationalize the decision.

My doctor told me that society would accept me as a single mom, and I would be able to afford it. But he didn't discuss the pregnancy in terms of the baby's development nor did he discuss the procedure with me. He didn't refer me to an abortion clinic, so to me it seemed less like an abortion.

EMPTY ARMS

My boyfriend drove me to the appointment. A nurse gave me Valium, and the doctor performed a suction abortion. I cried during the whole thing, thinking I could have said, "Stop!"

The minute it was over, I wailed, "Why did he make me kill my baby?"

When we left the doctor's office, we went directly to a church. My boyfriend waited in the car and could not understand the sorrow that overwhelmed me. A few weeks after the abortion, he left our relationship. We just responded to the experience too differently.

I discovered I had traded one problem for a host of others. Only in hindsight did I realize that our relationship was all about sex and nothing about love. I was depressed for a long time and felt that I blew my one chance at motherhood. I see myself as undeserving to be a mother, because I already proved that I'm a terrible mother. My family doesn't know about my abortion. I am afraid of the possibility of rejection. Each year around the anniversary of my abortion, I get depressed and moody. And the birth date of my baby makes me intensely sad. I will always remember my baby, my only child.

I have chosen to remember my baby at the National Memorial for the Unborn, and I named him David Matthew. I am grateful to have a place to honor him, and I hope The Memorial will one day stand as a reminder to society that abortion is about much more than a matter of choice.

—Donna T.

May the LORD keep watch between you and
me when we are away from each other.
Genesis 31:49

BABY GRACE
October 1986
I Am So Sorry—Someday in Heaven

I was thirteen when I first got pregnant. That seems young to me now, but then I felt old. I grew up fast. My parents were alcoholics and spent the majority of their time with their drinking buddies. Their closest friends had a son my age. I remember the first time we went too far. Before long we were having sex whenever we could. I had been taught that premarital sex was okay, and I had seen it done in a hundred different ways on TV, but deep down I still knew it was wrong. Every time was going to be our last time, but we always ended up doing it again. I just wanted to be loved so badly.

When my home pregnancy test turned up positive, we were scared, and I was numb. We never discussed abortion, and we made plans for a baby. We never wanted to get rid of our child, just the shame of having one. I was almost four months pregnant when I finally told my mom. I couldn't face her so I left a note in her car.

My mother's reaction confirmed my fears. What would people think? What about school? She said she thought she could trust me. We decided abortion was the answer. And we saw a counselor who assured me I was making a responsible decision; she referred me to Planned Parenthood.

Because I was in the second trimester, I had to go to a clinic out of town. The staff members were very supportive and even made the whole ordeal sound like fun.

"Go into the city, and shop while you are there," one said.

The abortion took a long time. I still remember the horrid sound of the aspirator as they sucked life from my womb. I screamed the entire time. The doctor yelled at the nurse to give me another shot.

"Do you want to go home pregnant?" he asked me. "Grow up!"

They filled glass jars with blood, and I saw something white floating in one. Was that my child?

In the months that followed, I spent all my spare time alone in my room. My mom became concerned and took me back to Planned Parenthood. They counseled me to get a kitten, and then refused to see me after that. I felt so empty and wished I could go back and change things. For years I lived with inner turmoil and hated myself for what I had done. But I cared more about what people thought of me than the truth. Abortion had spared me the initial shame of people finding out I was pregnant, but now shame and guilt were slowly destroying me.

When I had a baby at sixteen, that relieved some of my guilt but not the emptiness. I finished high school, got married, and finished college. Some time later, after being a Christian for a while, a Christian doctor heard my confession. Later, I read an article by Dr. James Dobson about the Israelites in the Old Testament who sacrificed their children to idols. That's when I realized I had done the same thing: I had sacrificed my child on the altar of selfishness.

I still deeply regret the choice I made almost twelve years ago. If I could, I would go back and bear the embarrassment that would have lasted but a short time. I no longer want to remain silent. I want to shout to the world that abortion is wrong. It is murder. It not only takes an innocent life but harms all of those involved. You can't cover the shame. You have to take it to the cross.

—Jolinda Lynch

It is by the name of Jesus Christ of Nazareth, whom you crucified but whom God raised from the dead, that this man stands before you healed. He is "the stone you builders rejected, which has become the capstone." Salvation is found in no one else, for there is no other name under heaven given to men by which we must be saved.
Acts 4:10–12

> # JEREMIAH PAUL
> January 22, 1993
> *I'll Always Love You. Hold You Soon . . . Mom*
>

When I found out I was pregnant, I was shocked, devastated, and scared to death. I'd never felt so desperate and alone, and was in no condition emotionally and hormonally to make a major decision. I was under mental torment and had tunnel vision.

The worst part is I was always Pro-Life and vowed never to have an abortion. Ironically, the day of my abortion was the twentieth anniversary of *Roe v. Wade*. A part of me died along with my baby that day. Deep down I wanted that baby so badly, but I just couldn't see a way out. I left the clinic with a heaviness that escalated over the next year. The minute the abortion was over, I agonized that I could not change it. I regretted it and would have given anything to have my baby back. I became depressed and seriously suicidal. I acted as normal as I could around my friends, but inside I felt guilty, hopeless, and grieved for my child.

Since I've come back to Jesus, He's changed me so much. He is a God of restoration, and I've experienced His healing power.

It took a long time for me to take the steps of forgiveness, but God met me where I was and went with me every step of the way. I am grateful to place a plaque in memory of my child. It helps put closure on my past. It's comforting to know he is memorialized. A marker indicates that he was here, if only for a short time.

—Anonymous

This is what the LORD says: "Let not the wise man boast of his wisdom or the strong man boast of his strength or the rich man boast of his riches, but let him who boasts boast about this: that he understands and knows me."
Jeremiah 9:23, 24

> **SARA ANN SCHUBERT**
> March 1972
> *Daddy's Little Girl*

> **RACHEL MARIE DISHAW**
> October 15, 1973
> *Forever a Part of Our Lives*

I was seventeen years old, a senior in high school. Mike had already graduated from high school, and we were in love. A part of me wanted to get pregnant; I wanted to be a part of his warm loving, family. But when it happened, reality set in, and I was in a crisis.

We were both afraid to tell our parents, and I confided in a teacher, who suggested I have an abortion. Even though I told him Mike wanted to marry me and have the baby, his counsel was that I was too young to get married and be tied down. He did encourage me to tell my parents about the pregnancy, though.

My parents were very upset and argued about whose side of the family I took after. Nobody wanted to claim me. They were more concerned about what people would think than they were about me and the baby, and this put a strain on our relationship for years.

My parents told me I had two choices: get married now or have an abortion. They were angry at Mike and wouldn't let him come over or talk to me on the phone, so he and I never really discussed the situation with anyone. Someone gave us information about abortion (in 1972, it was illegal). Within a couple of days, I was on a plane to New York City all by myself.

Before I left, I called Mike, and he begged me not to do it. He said he wanted the baby and would raise it himself. I told him it was too late. He called a lawyer to see if he could stop me from ending the life of the child he wanted so desperately. The plaque for this child reads "Daddy's Little Girl." I gave her his last name.

I got pregnant again one year later, and because of the damage done during the first abortion, my doctor ordered a therapeutic abortion. Later through prayer, God revealed to me that this was a girl, and I named her Rachel Marie. I later married Rachel's father. I found myself in deep denial, trying to pretend that the abortions never happened. If I picked up a magazine or newspaper and saw the word *abortion*, I would get rid of it. If I heard the word on the radio, I would turn it off.

My husband was verbally and physically abusive to me, and I was admitted to a psychiatric hospital for depression and malnutrition. During my six-week stay, I was able to work through the rape I had experienced as a child and the accidental death of my brother. But I never mentioned my two abortions.

My marriage ended in divorce when my sons were three and one and I was spiritually empty. One day I realized I was the mother of four children and surrendered my life to Jesus Christ. The guilt was drowning me, and I knew I needed help.

Soon after giving my life to Christ, I met my husband Jim. Together we found a wonderful Bible-teaching church, and I entered a support group. I was a broken woman whose heart ached to hold the children that died as a result of my sins. Jim adopted my boys and my sacrificed daughter Rachel, and I gave her his last name. In the spring of 1990, I located Mike and asked for his forgiveness. This played a big part in my healing. My parents and I have mended our relationship and are very close. We are now all members of the family of Christ.

—Sharon Dishaw

For you have been born again, not of perishable seed, but of imperishable, through the living and enduring word of God.
1 Peter 1:23

WILLIAM GLEN CANN
1981
"The Truth Shall Set You Free"

My husband and I had four children—three boys and one girl. My daughter was a lovely person and gave so much of herself to others. Because of a lack of real bonding with her father, she entered a relationship with a young man and became pregnant. I found out about her abortion after the fact. Sadness gripped my heart, but there was nothing I could say or do. So I accepted the problem and went on with my life.

Later, our daughter became pregnant again, but this time she chose to have the baby. Before my husband's death in 1987, he and I helped raise our granddaughter Katie together for four years. She is now twenty-one, a beautiful, radiant girl with an outgoing personality, blonde hair, and blue eyes. I can't imagine life without her. My daughter is now happily married with five other children.

When Katie's father originally suggested an abortion, my daughter said no. I am so thankful she put God first, because Katie is a beautiful, responsible child who loves her siblings. My prayers as a mother and grandmother were answered, and I continue to be grateful for God's hand of mercy and grace.

—Mary Louise Cann

Jesus said, "If you hold to my teaching ... Then you will know the truth and the truth will set you free."
John 8:31, 32

HAMILTON LEE
1980
If I Only Knew... Mom

I grew up in a home with three brothers and two sisters. My father was an abusive alcoholic. My mother cared for us and provided for us since my father was not home most of the time. At the age of fifteen, I got involved with a boy and became pregnant. I just wanted out of the house and to live on my own.

I had my first child at sixteen, and by the time I was twenty, I had four children and was still single. After being involved in many abusive relationships, I became pregnant again. I knew that as a single woman, I was doing well to raise the four I had already. So a doctor told me it was just a blob of tissue at this stage, and I could abort if I wanted to. He told me where I could get the abortion. You always trust your doctor to give you the correct information. So I talked it over with my friends, and they thought abortion would be the best thing to do. I was having a hard time as it was, without adding another child. A friend drove me to Atlanta, and I had the abortion.

I thought that this would end my problems, but little did I know, they had just begun. One year later, I had to have a hysterectomy, and I had just met the man I was going to marry. He had never been married and did not have children. But I had to have this done, or I might have died. After we got married, I put all this out of my mind and pushed it so far down that only I knew why I hurt so badly. Twenty years later, after my first grandson was born, I realized that the baby I had aborted was just that, a baby.

By this time, I had given my life to the Lord and attended a Bible study, "Forgiven and Set Free." That was the best thing I had ever done other than accepting the Lord Jesus as my Savior.

By the end of the study, I was forgiven and set free from the pain of that abortion. I am now involved with women who want to choose abortion and pray that I can help them to give life instead of taking it away. What the devil meant for evil, God has used for good.

—Wanda King

Rend your heart and not your garments.
Return to the L<small>ORD</small> *your God, for he is gracious*
and compassionate, slow to anger and abounding
in love, and he relents from sending calamity.
Joel 2:13

AMY—MY LOVE
March 8, 1973
You Always Lived in My Heart

I had two babies prematurely. The doctor told us it was too risky to have any more children, so my husband had a vasectomy. We were Christians and faithful churchgoers. I don't know why I didn't see trouble ahead. I asked my husband for a divorce because I thought I was in love with another man. We stayed in our marriage because of the children, and I knew that what I was doing was wrong.

The other relationship ended, but I saw the other man again and became pregnant the week of January 22, 1973, the week abortion was legalized. I wanted the baby, but I was mixed up and confused. When I told my husband, he was broken up over my actions, but he didn't encourage or discourage an abortion. Somehow in my reasoning, I thought having an abortion would make things okay again.

I cried during the abortion. The nurse thought I was in pain, but it wasn't physical pain. That night when the sedative wore off, I wanted to die. After that, at parks or children's events I mourned the baby I had aborted and couldn't fully appreciate the children I did have. Not a day goes by that I do not wish I had my baby. Several years ago, I went through Post Abortion Counseling and Education (PACE). What a burden has been lifted! I placed a plaque at The Memorial for the Unborn on dedication day, which was the best thing I've ever done. I now have a place to go, remember my child, and hope for the day I will see her in heaven.

—Anonymous

Who is a God like you, who pardons sin and forgives the transgression . . . of his inheritance? You do not stay angry forever but delight to show mercy. You will again have compassion on us; you will tread our sins underfoot and hurl all our iniquities into the depths of the sea.
Micah 7:18, 19

MY PRECIOUS BABY MATTHEW
August 1984
I Hold You in My Heart Daily

I was raised a Christian but at the age of twenty I started to doubt God. My parents' relationship was bad and my mother was suicidal. I started to hang around with non-believers. During this time, I met a guy who pressured me to have sex with him. So I went to Planned Parenthood and started on the pill which I thought was safe. We only had sex once, and six weeks later I was pregnant. I stopped seeing him. Planned Parenthood thought it was best for me to have an abortion so I could go on with my life and not embarrass my family.

I scheduled the abortion, and I remember how cold everyone was.

"Just bring three hundred dollars in cash or a cashier's check."

The day I walked into the clinic, a Pro-Life group was picketing outside. I prayed one of them would stop me and say everything would be okay, and that they would help me with the baby. Instead they called me a murderer. I didn't see the Lord at work in any of them. And afterwards when I came out they were still yelling at me. No one asked, "Can I help you?"

After that my whole life went downhill. I was cold, selfish, hateful, enraged. I cut myself off from all my friends and turned away from God. I started to have sexual relationships with every man I met. Then I moved on to married men. I didn't think they or anyone had the right to have a happy, respectful relationship. I was caught for shoplifting and spent a night in jail. I used drugs and alcohol.

Then I met a man I didn't really care for. I went out with him for a free meal. He had just given his life to the Lord and helped to start me on my walk as well. He was supportive, and suggested I take a PACE class at his church. One month later, we started dating and then decided to get married. He supported me and wasn't judgmental, and we now have three beautiful daughters.

I now work at a crisis pregnancy center and teach PACE for the clinic. In 1996 during a trip to the National Convention in Tennessee, I knew that God was saying that it was time to put my baby to rest. It was the hardest thing to do, but it was God's timing and an answer to prayer. A plaque has been placed in his honor at the National Memorial for the Unborn. I now have peace.

—Holly Lewis

"The thief comes only to steal and kill and destroy; I have come that they may have life, and have it to the full."
John 10:10

CATHERINE
May 1, 1984
I'll Hold You in Heaven

I was a young lady with a desire to wait until I got married to have sex. But at the age of thirteen all that was taken away by rape. This horrible experience exposed me to the world of sex. My life was a mess. At age twenty-one I was still looking for love that I could not find at home. I met a man at work, went to his apartment, and we had sex.

Soon after that I found out I was pregnant. I was in a state of shock. I told the father and he responded by saying, "I don't know you, that baby is not mine, don't ever talk to me again." He told me I was just a one-night stand.

My heart was broken and I thought of killing myself. My mother's response was, "You can't keep this baby, you are too young. You have the rest of your life ahead of you. Get an abortion."

So my mother and I went to the abortion clinic where I chose to give up the life inside of me. I went into deep depression and started to run from my problems. It was then that I ran into Jesus. I went through Post Abortion Counseling and Education (PACE) where I forgave the man who raped me, forgave the father of the baby, and forgave my mother. I also prayed and asked God to forgive me for taking my daughter's life.

During the memorial service for Catherine I released all my pain and released Catherine into the hands of God. Knowing my child's name is on The Wall gives me hope and a desire to see The Memorial.

—Teressa

*"Do not let your hearts be troubled.
Trust in God; trust also in me."*
John 14:1

"Do you not know that your body is a temple of the Holy Spirit, who is in you, whom you have received from God? You are not your own; you were bought at a price. Therefore honor God with your body."
1 Corinthians 6:19, 20

EMMANUEL JOY
December 1983 – January 1984
Psalm 34:5

I was twenty-one years old, a senior in college, with my whole life ahead of me. I had goals, dreams, and had even studied one and a half years abroad. In December during Christmas break, I got pregnant. Like many girls I was looking for love in all the wrong places. In January 1984, one month later, I had an abortion.

The month between pregnancy and abortion was a time of extreme crisis. My goals! My dreams! No money! I sought counsel from a nursing student, who said, "It's just a blob of tissue." I sought counsel from clergy at my church, and she said, "Whatever you decide, God will understand." Society, a family member, and all but one friend said abortion was the way. One friend said, "If you choose abortion, God won't like it." I hung up on her. My heart was like stone.

You see, I sought God on my terms then. I didn't know Him as personal Savior and Lord. I knew Him as some benevolent power out there that I talked to and would journal to, at my convenience.

That day in January turned my life to death. The day I killed my child, I died, too. I turned my back on any understanding I had of God—a black cloud hung over me. I never knew abortion would do that. And like most, I was so deceived

I never related it to the abortion. Although I had all the outward appearances of success—a home, nice car, excellent career, and a good looking boyfriend—I became self-abusive and went from one abusive male relationship to another.

In May of 1988, I went to videotape the birth of my first niece. My sister and brother-in-law had come to know the Lord shortly before. When I saw the birth of that precious little baby girl so perfect, a miracle, something inside me changed and I knew somewhere there was a God who loved me—a perfect God, a Creator.

I went back home to the abusive relationship and that Christmas my sister sent me a Bible. I read that Bible and searched it for answers. When the abuse was the worst, the Bible brought me comfort.

In June of 1987, I was almost killed in that relationship. From the bottom of the pit God rescued me. I left that night. I called my sister and brother-in-law to see if I could live with them. They said without hesitation, "Our home is God's home and you are welcome, but you will have to go to church every Sunday." That was no problem for me. I was looking for God and I liked the God I saw in them.

On June 13 I moved to Portland, Oregon, and on June 14 I accepted Jesus Christ as my Lord and Savior—on His terms, under His Lordship. I received immediate transformation from darkness to light. That night while praying at the end of my bed God showed me what I had done to my baby—His creation for whom He had a purpose. In His understanding, He waited until I was in His loving arms to show me what I had done. I asked His forgiveness and it was granted that night.

Slowly, but surely, the shame that consumed me was brought into His light. Through a Bible study support group at the local crisis pregnancy center, I dealt with the hidden anger, shame, and depression that was destroying me. The secrecy of my abortion kept me distant from my parents, family, and most significantly, God. It was hard for me to trust. Secrets harden our heart. Through the Word of God, prayer, and a faithful support group I was able to forgive others and myself. God truly turned my heart of stone into a heart of flesh and gave me a new spirit.

Today, I am the director of HEART (Healing Encouragement for Abortion Related Trauma), based in Portland, Oregon, a ministry of the Portland Crisis Pregnancy Center. We assist men and women suffering from abortion's aftermath. We use *Forgiven and Set Free* (formerly known as PACE: Women in Ramah) authored by Linda Cochrane. I have been helping people with post-abortion stress (PAS) through Bible study support groups since February 1988. This is when I began my personal journey from shame to grace. The shame isn't gone through one group session but a huge layer is peeled away, like an onion. When I peel an onion, I cry. Every time I share my testimony with either one person or 6,000 (in the U.S., Russia, Kazakstan, and Eastern Europe), another layer is peeled away and God is given glory! What Satan meant for my destruction, God redeemed, so I have been able to minister for His glory.

I heard about the National Memorial for the Unborn in Chattanooga but did not have the money to place a plaque there in memory of my child. When I went through the PACE program in 1996, we went to The Memorial. It was then that the burden in my heart began. The plaque would be another step in bringing honor and dignity to Emmanuel Joy. My heart cried for the millions of grandparents, siblings, cousins, and fathers who had no place to face their loss. I went back to Portland with this burden and shared it with my father, Emmanuel's grandfather. He, being a World War II veteran and a man of the 1940s and 50s, didn't seem to get it. But two hours later as we were saying good-bye, he said, "How much is that plaque you mentioned? I would like to pay for that plaque in memory of my granddaughter." And a tear welled up in his eye. Today a plaque shines bright in Chattanooga in memory of Emmanuel.

A group of Pro-Life advocates in Portland plan to establish an affiliate Memorial site. Their mission statement is, "The Northwest Memorial for the Unborn is a Christ-centered ministry devoted to the sanctity of human life, the healing of families and the memory of babies lost to abortion" which reflects the mission of the National Memorial.

—Athlynn Reeves

Those who look to him are radiant;
their faces are never covered with shame.
Psalm 34:5

> # Mis Bebes Preciosos
> ## (My Precious Babies)
> February 24, 2006
>
>

My Dear Dale Andres, Ramon Rafael, Haydee Rosario, all of you,

How incredible it is for me to be able to write you this letter, to be able to talk to you for the first time in my life. You may be asleep at this time, but I know some day these words will reach you. The first words I speak to you as your mother. I like to think that God is allowing you, together with my mother, to listen to them.

It feels so wonderful to call you mine. It is like I am touching you, and you have again become a part of me. You are my precious babies, and I don't hide you in my heart anymore. How to explain all the emotions I feel in a single letter.

The first thing I want to say to you is that I am sorry. I am sorry that the place that should have been the safest became the most dangerous one for you. Nobody is to blame but myself.

My sweet precious babies, what happened did not happen because you were not lovable and precious and beautiful. Each one of you are a blessing from God–a beautiful little angel that now again touches and blesses my life. You are beautifully and wonderfully made and I love you.

I have always been afraid of getting to heaven and

seeing you because I did not know what would happen...would you forgive me? Would you love me?

Oh, my babies, we have the hope of heaven. At the sound of the trumpet, on our journey to be with Jesus forever. We will embrace, we will kiss, we will love and we will have an eternity together. My arms long to hold you. My arms that are hungry for your touch and your love...praise to my Lord Jesus, will be full of you one day.

From this day forward we walk together. I don't hide you in my heart any longer. Wherever I go, you go with me. See and watch all the wonderful ways God is going to use US together as the little family that we are, to bring light and healing to many souls. Oh, my sweets, in heaven someday we will rejoice seeing how God used our testimony; because it is ours, to save and heal many grieving souls. Together you and I always...sharing our tears and joys for the glory of God! You, my children, have become my beautiful picture...

Let me pray for us...it is so wonderful to be able to do it...

Oh my Jesus, thank you for returning to me that which was stolen. Bless us and use us for your glory, that my children and I can become something that brings hope and light into darkness. Thank you for blessing my children, thank you for the hope of heaven. Thank you for being my God. Thank you for my babies and thank you for healing our hearts.

My sweet little children, soon you will be in my arms...I love you with all my heart, with all my love...Mami

To appoint unto them that mourn in Zion, to give unto them beauty for ashes, the oil of joy for mourning, the garment of praise for the spirit of heaviness; that they might be called trees of righteousness, the planting of the Lord, that he might be glorified.
Isaiah 61:3

SKYLAR
1995
Matthew 6:33

To my precious Skylar,

Skylar, my sweet baby, I am here tonight to remember and honor you. I am sorry it has taken so long, but rejoice, knowing that God has brought me to this place along with my sisters in Christ.

You were a tremendous part of me for 12 weeks and you have been for 20 years, but I did not realize how much until a few weeks ago. I will never ignore you again, but will remember you, love you, and honor you. You do live, you live in my heart, in my mind, and with Jesus. You were safe with me for a little while, but I did not keep you safe as a mother should. You are God's creation that is loved and wanted.

I find comfort knowing that you are completely whole and perfect in heaven. I feel so much love for you, even though I never held you in my arms or saw your sweet face. Skylar, I miss you and look forward to the day when my entire family will meet you and live forever in the presence of our mighty God. Maybe I will have the chance to hear you say "Mama."

If I could take back what I did to you, I would! I am so sorry. You would be 20 years old now, but I stopped short the miracle of your development. I want you to know that you would have been loved by so many people.

Through God's grace and mercy I will be joining you one day. God has forgiven me and I have moved past the guilt and shame in order to be useful to God and bring you honor. I have let go of the guilt, but I still grieve over you. I am forgiven, but I will not forget you.

May your presence in my world compel me to be a light to the hurting and may God use our story to bring glory to the King. I love you and until I see you, my precious child, I will honor you. I pray that I will follow our Lord as He guides me to be useful to His Kingdom.

Skylar, this is not the end for us, it is a new beginning.

Love you,
Mama

But seek ye first the Kingdom of God and His righteousness and all these things shall be added unto you.
Matthew 6:33

JEREMY
November 30, 2013
Our Darkest Day

Jeremy,
Mommy and Daddy are mournfully sorry for our actions. Daddy has tried to forget that day, but the reality of it is too real. Mommy has helped me get in touch with my emotions and feelings about it. Growing up in this world as a man, there is a lot of pressure to tuck emotions and feelings deep down inside and never expose them. This is not a trait of a strong man, it is a trait of a weak man. I was blinded in my darkest moment by my own selfishness and preoccupations. It has been over a year since that day and your mother and I have shed many tears. It's a father's role to protect and provide for his children and significant other. I failed you and for that I am deeply sorry. I have gained a deeper relationship with God over the past year and I see a lot of truths in His words. I know that you're up there with Him now, looking down on Mommy and I. We both want you to know that we are very sorry and regret ever doing it. Your mother is a sweet nurturing woman and loves you with all of her heart.

Jeremy, son, Mommy and Daddy love you and we are painfully sorry. Mommy and Daddy are sorry, son. We love you and pray to see you one day in heaven.

–Dad

Come to me, all you who labor and are burdened, and I will give you rest. Take my yoke upon you and learn from me, for I am meek and humble of heart and you will find rest for your souls. For my yoke is easy and my burden light.
Matthew 11:28-30

Poems from the Wall

My Little One, Where Are You?

Oh, how I miss you! My arms are so empty.
I long to hold you. My heart weeps unseen
tears because you are not here.

How can it be that I'll never see your
dimpled cheeks and bright eyes?
My dreams for you are shattered.
I really wanted to protect you and take care of you . . .
but now you are gone.

Oh, my baby, I miss you so! I am so empty.
My heart is heavy with grief.

Please, I need to know where you are right now . . .

"The Lord God will gather the lambs with His
arm and carry them in His bosom."

Your baby is snuggled in the strong, but gentle arms of the Good Shepherd, Jesus. What a secure and precious place to be!

—Mareta Keener Thomas

(entire page used by permission)

HELP! (A Memorial to My Child)

"Help!" I cried. "I'm pregnant. Help! Help!"
"I'll help you," he said. "You'll have an abortion;
and no one will know.
Here's my half of the fee.
Now go; and never mention this again."

"Help!" I cried. "I'm sinking.
Life is overwhelming me.
I'm lost. Help!"
"Here I AM," said God.
"I will introduce you to my Son.
He will save you and help you.
He is the Way, the Truth and the Life."

"Help! Help!
Somebody, help me!
My baby is gone.
Oh, where is my baby?
He's gone.
Oh, he's gone.
I cannot go on.
No, I cannot.
Oh, help me, God, or I will go crazy!"

"I AM here, my child.
I promised I would never leave you nor forsake you.
I will turn your mourning into dancing and your sackcloth
    into gladness.
I love you, my child.

I AM here.
I will always be here."

"Help! I'm still sad. Help!"
"My child, you are forgiven.
Accept your forgiveness.
Go and sin no more.
Your child is in heaven.
You will be together someday."

Thank you, Lord, for helping me.
I love you so much, dear Lord.
Thank you for giving my child back to me.
I shall meet him in heaven someday.

Dedicated to Dana M.
Winter 1964 —By his loving Mom

Mommy

I dreamt I went to heaven, and there in front of me
    stood wildflowers in a valley gently blowing by the breeze.
I bent down and picked one and brought it to my nose,
    but to my surprise it suddenly began to change and grow.

To my amazement, it developed into a perfect little child.
Its eyes looked deep into my soul; its voice spoke meek
    and mild.
"Dear lady, have you seen my mother down on earth?
She's a beautiful woman who was too afraid to give me birth.

And so I ask each one who passes through these flowers as
    they go
in hopes that someday it will be she I'll come to know."
With the shake of my head, the baby disappointedly
    looked away
and quietly, so quietly this precious child began to pray.

"Holy Father, please forgive her with your mercy and
    your grace
so that someday we will be reunited in these heavens face
    to face.
Let her broken heart cry out for you, let her spirit be set free
    from all the shame and torment so that she can hold me."

Tears began to fall down from my repented eyes.
"Are all these flowers children who have lost their lives?"
"Yes," the child nodded, "I'm sad to say it's so.
There are too many to count and ponder . . .
I know, I know . . .

"But each one of us has his own special story,
    and we believer that God will use us for His glory,
That our deaths will help somehow to bring our mothers
    to their knees
to call upon the risen Savior who died for you and me."

The child climbed down from my arms and slowly walked
    over to its appointed place
turning back into the flower that I had picked, with still a
    smile upon its face.
My mind began to wonder, my time there had been
    completed.
Yet the child's voice echoed through my spirit, and it pleaded.

"As you awake from dreaming, dear lady, don't forget me.
Please help me, Lord, help me find my mommy . . ."

(Dedicated to the 35 million children who have perished on the altar of abortion since it was made "legal" on January 22, 1973. One, I'm sorry to say, was my child.)

—Heidi Hetsteck
Kalamazoo, Michigan

EMPTY ARMS

THIS CHILD OF MINE

This child of mine,
The child I never knew,
This is in remembrance
Of the time I carried you.

Though you were ever present,
You had no earthly voice.
That chance had been denied
Because the world gave me a choice.

And now as I look back,
A painful loss in you I find;
And the guilt of my denial
Has overtaken heart and mind.

I must ask you for forgiveness,
As I lay you here to rest.
Know that had I not been blinded
By the world, I would be blessed.

There's one thing that I promise you,
Since God has set me free,
Though in heaven you rest without me,
In my heart you will always be.

Dedicated with love to Jason Dane Vadala,
    son of Jeanne Elaine Vadala
    conceived May 1979, died July 1979

—Written May 22, 1995, by his mother

Can't Cry for My Baby

I wake up and know what I've done.
I grab someone's arm,
"Please, was it a boy or a girl?"
She's angry.
"It's just a piece of tissue. No way to know!"

I need to get away from here.
If I can get out of here and get home,
I can put it all behind me and forget about it.
I've erased my past. I can start over.
Just have to get away from this place.

So I smile. I pretend I'm fine now.
"I want to go home. No really, I feel fine.
I'll be fine. Just need to go home."

Will the cab driver know what I've done?
I paste a smile on my face.
Pretend I'm the same as when I went in.
Just visiting, you know.

I make it home, smile at the woman in the lobby—
"Got off early from work today."
"That's nice."
I hurt, I feel sick.
My face is hot with shame.
Can't they see what I've done?

I'm back in the safety of my room.
I cannot think about this.

I've erased it all, and I'm going to start all over.
I see an eraser, moving back and forth,
erasing my baby.
Other pictures take over.
Blood, violence, death, baby parts, a cry,
white, sterile environment,
smiling nurse, angry nurse.
I can't face these pictures in my head.
I need a drink.
I need to sleep.
Need to not think about it.

I wonder what they did with my baby?
Shut up! I can't think about this now!

Have to go to work tomorrow.
Have to pretend everything's okay.
I *did not* just have an abortion!
Just felt a little under the weather last week.
I'm fine now.
I paste a smile on my face.
But I'm empty inside.
I'm so, so empty inside.
I want to cry deep wracking sobs.

"Surely you're not going to cry for your baby! You killed it!
What a hypocrite!
You're a murderer!"

But I can't stop the tears.
So I cry but not for my baby.
I just cry for no reason at all.

I've turned my back on God.
Can't face him with what I've done.
He's angry
I made this choice.
Can't ever go back.
No use thinking about it.
"There's no way back."
My baby would have been born today.
I start to feel the loss,
but I can't think about it now.
I'm getting married in three days.
Why am I crying? Can't cry for my baby.
I cry for no reason at all.
It's time to pretend I'm a happy bride. I smile.

My baby would have her (his?) first birthday tomorrow.
Would she be walking now?
Haven't thought about this in a while.
It hurts. I killed my baby. I want to die.
"Why don't you then?
You should kill yourself.
You don't deserve to live!"
"I know, but I'm afraid. I'm afraid of hell."

"You weren't afraid to kill your baby.
Why get cold feet now?
You're not just a murderer,
You're selfish and cowardly.
You killed your own baby without a qualm,
But you're afraid to kill yourself.
You're pathetic!"

EMPTY ARMS

My baby would be four today.
Would she be excited about Christmas?
Would we make cookies together?
Put red ribbons in her hair?
Why am I thinking about this now?
My anniversary is in three days.
No one would understand.
I have to pretend everything's okay.
Don't think about it.
Don't think about it!
Can't cry for my baby.

What's your problem?
He hit you? So what? You deserve it.
At least he didn't kill you.
You killed your baby.
You deserve a lot worse.

Did my baby feel pain?
Can't think about it.
Can't cry for my baby.

I'm divorced.
Alone, relieved, rejected, afraid,
Loneliness, relief, rejection
What now???

I've pretended too long.
I don't even really exist.
I'm just pretending.

I don't think about my baby much anymore.

EMPTY ARMS

My heart is cold,
a block of ice.
I'm in "Night of the Living Dead."
A zombie
Pretending to exist.

Sometimes I think about God.
I know my way is death and God is life.
But I've gone too far.
No way to get back.
Some sins are *unforgivable*.

God has mercy on me.
He finds me through the fog, the darkness,
The hard shell I'm hiding in.
Into my darkness He shines His light.
He woos me and loves me and
draws me to Himself.

God, I killed my baby. Will you forgive me?
Why don't I feel grief? I must be a monster.
I don't feel anything. *My heart is stone.*

Susan Smith pushes her children to a watery grave
and lies about it.
The whole town is enraged.
How could she do that?
"*You are that woman!*" No!

I can't *not think about it* any more.
I think about it all the time.
I'm falling apart.

God still cares. He brings me to a place of healing.
He said: "I will sprinkle clean water on you,
and you will be clean; I will cleanse you from all
your impurities ... I will remove from you your
heart of stone and give you a heart of flesh."

I accept Jesus' death as payment for my sin.
He removes my heart of stone.
My baby was *not* a piece of tissue.
She was *not* a choice.
She was a precious child created in the
image of God,
loved by Him,
valued by Him.
Waves of grief flow through me.

I cry for my baby.
She lived for a short time inside me,
now she's gone.
I love her. I want her. My arms are empty.
She will not return to me, but I will go to her.
I'll hold her in heaven.

Her name is Callie Anna Watts.
Anna means grace. Through my precious child,
I learned of God's grace to me.
When the Accuser confronts me, my baby's name
reminds me of God's grace,
mercy,
forgiveness,
infinite love.

EMPTY ARMS

His grace is greater than all my sin . . .
Oh, amazing grace, how sweet the sound.

A fragrant garden removes the stench of death.
Beauty for ashes
An Ebenezer stone.
A granite wall.
A memorial plaque.
After twelve years of shame and guilt,
I bring my baby out of the dark
and into the light.
Her name is placed on The Wall of Names.
Dignity, honor, value, worth.
She will not be forgotten,
Others will mourn her death with me.
She will be remembered in this place of healing,
and always in my heart,
until—*I hold her in heaven.*

—Carolyn Rice

For I know my transgressions, and my sin is always before me. . . . Blot out all my iniquity. Create in me a pure heart, O God, and renew a steadfast spirit within me. Do not cast me from your presence or take your Holy Spirit from me. Restore to me the joy of your salvation and grant me a willing spirit, to sustain me.
Psalm 51:3, 9–12

Cries from the Cradle
Stories of Adoption

Introduction
by Wendy Williams

Although I have not personally experienced an abortion, my husband and I have experienced deep grief in losing many babies. This sense of aching to hold a newborn drew us to be involved with The National Memorial for the Unborn. Yet ours is a different grief because it is tempered with joy.

For over seventeen years, we have provided shelter in our home to both women in crisis pregnancies and foster babies through Bethany Christian Services, a private, nonprofit, licensed, Christian social-service agency. This group is part of a large network of organizations that provides pregnancy testing, free counseling, medical care, clothing, and housing to hurting women in order to encourage them to choose an adoption plan or parenting over abortion. These groups have paid staffs but rely heavily on volunteers to aid in mending broken lives and offering hope for the women in crisis.

Henry and I felt called to this ministry because of the opportunity we had to see God work in my family. I was in college when my younger sister ran away from home. She had just graduated from high school. My parents felt as if they were living a nightmare. For two years she wandered, calling occasionally at holidays when she was lonely. One person told my father he should disown her, but he replied, "God loves us no matter what, so I will continue to let her know we love her." His response reminds me of the verse where the Lord says, "I have loved you with an everlasting love" (Jeremiah 31:3).

Finally, in answer to our prayers, she arrived home. But she only planned to stay long enough to tell our parents she was pregnant and then was returning to the commune where she was living in California. Again, the Lord heard our prayers, for three times she tried to leave but was delayed by the flu, painful wisdom teeth, and car trouble. This gave us the opportunity to convince her to stay with her family. During her pregnancy, a group of Christians showed their love and concern for her and the baby she was carrying. When your family is in a crisis, it is such a blessing to have others come alongside to encourage and share your burdens.

My sister began to read the Bible and came upon a passage that spoke to her:

> With what shall I come before the LORD? . . . Shall I offer my firstborn for my transgression . . . ? What does the LORD require of you? To act justly and to love mercy and to walk humbly with your God (Micah 6:6–8).

These verses helped her to realize that an abortion was not the answer to her problem, and the Lord desired a relationship with her. With loving support, she chose to keep her child and commit their lives to the Lord. She named her son Micah. She later married a man she met in her church who adopted her son. The Lord blessed them with three other children. My sister now volunteers to counsel other women to choose life for their babies.

Opening your home and family to serve is not without a price. Two of the most frequently asked questions are, "Won't you get attached?" and "How do you do it?" The answer from other foster mothers and our family is, Yes, you do get attached, and yes, your heart does break. There is no way you cannot miss that fuzzy-headed baby you rocked to sleep or that teenage girl who shared your table and helped you sing "Happy Birthday" to your child. But deep down you know it is worth the pain because you provided a place of shelter for a mother or infant while she made important, life-changing decisions. And you know that even if you never see them again, God will take care of them, and you can lift them up to Him in prayer.

Another foster family taught us the candle-lighting ceremony to bring closure when the baby is scheduled to leave. The Bible verse that brought comfort to me as we faced surrendering our beautiful little foster daughter was Hebrews 12:2, "Let us fix our eyes on Jesus . . . who for the joy set before him endured the cross." She had been in our home over four months, and that translates into hundreds of bottles, diapers, sleepless nights, and sweet smiles. Needless to say, it was painful to say good-bye. Now, years later after the adoption of our son, we have experienced the great joy of being on the receiving end.

We have had many healthy, normal babies who have transitioned smoothly. The following true stories are from some of the more difficult challenges we have had to face as foster parents. We share them to say that a choice for the life of the baby is not a quick fix but worth the pain. Rejoice with us in these encouraging episodes.

EMPTY ARMS

Clay

The phone rang a few days before Christmas. Could we take a tiny baby? Could we say no? How could there be "no room in the inn" at the Williams' home? After all, it was the holiday celebrating the day the Christ Child entered the world and needed a place to be born.

And that was what appeared to happen—Christ came into our home in the form of an olive-skinned, dark-haired baby boy. I cradled this little boy in my arms during the Christmas Eve service. My daughter picked the name Clay as his foster name. It made Christmas Day so much more meaningful to hear the tiny bleating cries of this newborn lamb.

The social worker told me only two details: he was Latino, and he had been exposed to drugs. I wondered if his placement would be long-term and an adoptive home hard to find because of his birth history.

We celebrated New Years' Day in our home with many relatives. My brother, a Lutheran minister, led us in a house blessing to dedicate our new home to the Lord. As owners, my husband and I held a lighted candle as we moved from room to room, the children trailing along, banging pots and pans to warn evil spirits to flee. Along with the extended family, we joined my brother in prayers designed specifically for the activities that would go on in each room. It was a sweet time of fellowship that ended in a communion service in the living room. Various family members prayed for our tiny visitor, Clay, asking God to provide him a new home. Only three weeks later, I dressed him in the most beautiful, all-white outfit provided by his new family as his going-home outfit.

Clay's family had been through some heart-wrenching situations. This young Christian couple had a baby boy, but he died only after a few days, and they couldn't take him home to the nursery decorated in Noah's ark wallpaper. Later, the mother gave birth to another son, but he lived only a month and died of similar birth defects as the first son.

The couple then heard of a teenager girl who led a wild life, became pregnant, and needed help. They offered to take her into their home, support her through her unplanned pregnancy, and adopt the baby even though the infant had been exposed to drugs. But after a while the girl ran away, so again their hopes were crushed. Instead of disappointing them, the Noah's ark wallpaper reminded them of Noah's God, who sent a rainbow to remind His people that He would have mercy. Three times this couple had a baby to love and raise, only to have the gift taken away. But they faced their hardships like Job: "The LORD gave and the LORD has taken away; may the name of the Lord be praised" (Job 1:21).

Finally, the couple filled out paperwork for adoption. When they got to the question, "Would you consider a drug-exposed baby?" they answered *yes* because they had already faced that with the last situation. So this couple was matched with our little Clay only one month after he came into our home. It was incredible to see how well the mother's coloring matched the baby's. Our prayers were answered and so were theirs.

What a beautiful picture—like God adopting us into His family. Ephesians 1:4–6 says, "For he chose us in him . . . to be holy and blameless in his sight. In love he predestined us to be adopted as his sons . . . to the praise of his glorious grace, which he has freely given us in the One he loves."

We have a new home we are enjoying, Clay has a new home with new parents he is enjoying, and someday, as we trust in Jesus, God will bring us to our new, eternal home in heaven to enjoy Him forever.

> *In my Father's house are many rooms;*
> *if it were not so, I would have told you.*
> *I am going there to prepare a place for you.*
> *And if I go and prepare a place for you,*
> *I will come back and take you to be with me*
> *that you also may be where I am.*
> John 14:2, 3

Luke

I had just returned from a ladies' Bible study at our church when the phone rang. A social worker called from Bethany, the adoption agency that supervised our family as the foster parents to a newborn we called Jesse. Gloria said she wanted us to pray about taking a another baby instead of Jesse. I quietly said I would pray, but my inner reaction was, *I don't want another baby. I have a sweet baby boy right now who we are enjoying.* This new baby was a difficult case. He had several serious medical problems that could be life threatening, so the social worker thought he should be in a doctor's home, and my husband was a doctor.

Henry and I prayed about it, then I called my brother for his opinion. He thoughtfully advised us to say no. He was concerned for our own four children and the trauma it would cause them to see a baby die. The poor baby had several strikes against him. I knew we would probably have him a long time because he didn't sound very adoptable. But that morning in church, I had told my friends how the Lord Jesus provided the right home for each foster baby we have had in our care over the years.

So I breathed a quick prayer and called Gloria back. We would keep both babies. We didn't want to miss out on the adoption of Jesse. The placement ceremony is always very special. It is what makes the sleepless nights and the heartaches worth the pain. To see a family receive the baby they have been longing for and now finally hold him in their arms is both our sorrow and our reward.

The next morning, I met Gloria at the hospital with Jesse in the car seat. The doctor explained the medical problems and the medications for the new baby. Then I went home with two baby boys, Jesse and Luke, both strapped in the back in two car seats. The next week was wild. I now have infinite respect for mothers of twins! My time was taken up with bottle feedings, burps, diaper changes, and dose after dose of medicine. My husband and two neighbors helped, but I handled the sick baby.

I was exhausted but experienced "the peace that passes all understanding." The Holy Spirit gave me the Scripture song from Psalm 42: "As the deer pants for streams of water, so my soul pants for you, O God." I sang that song many times to little Luke as I was up in the night feeding, changing, and giving him medications, and then trying to soothe him back to sleep. Among several problems were a subdural hematoma and open head wounds from a traumatic delivery that made him uncomfortable.

Our family affectionately called him "Wolfman" since he was born with beautiful olive skin and lots of dark, wavy hair. I actually gave him a haircut at two weeks of age. He was a sweet-natured, handsome little fellow, one of our favorite babies.

A nice couple adopted Jesse. He was a seemingly healthy baby, but he developed persistent vomiting shortly after his adoption. He had a pyloric stenosis and required surgery. I was amazed to think that I had cared for two medically fragile babies but didn't know it. I was thankful for God's mercy that the condition didn't manifest itself until after the adoption, so I didn't have to deal with both problems.

Luke seemed to grow a little stronger and more alert. He was coordinated at using his feet, and I was sure he'd be a soccer or basketball star if he ever got well.

After several weeks, I needed a break, and my friend was willing to take the risk of watching this sick baby. I walked into her front hall and set the baby in his car seat on the tile floor. I explained about the medicines and then said we didn't know if he would live or die. My friend, looking down at the sleeping infant, asked, "What will you do if he dies?" I tried to sound brave as I answered, "I guess we'll give him our last name and bury him." Then we both became teary at the prospect of one so tiny facing possible death.

Our social worker brought up the possibility of our adopting this baby. We prayed about it, but we already had four children, the last of which had special needs, so we said no.

Mary, my friend who helped me with the baby, had called us several weeks before wanting to borrow a copy of *Lifeline* magazine that publishes pictures of children waiting to be adopted. I had told her I had company for lunch and would look for it later, but she insisted that she and her family felt God was leading them to adopt, and they wanted the magazine right then.

Several weeks later, Mary told her tennis partner that their family felt God was leading them to adopt an older girl to fit in with their three birth daughters. But the friend asked, "What about adopting that sick baby the Williams have in their home?" Adopt an infant with medical problems? This hadn't occurred to them, but they began to pray about the possibility.

After they had decided this was the right decision, they realized that the day they asked for the adoption magazine was the very day little Luke came into this world. The Holy Spirit planted the thought of adoption in their hearts on his birthday.

When Mary told me they wanted to adopt Luke, I was amazed that they would even consider taking on such a risk.

EMPTY ARMS

Why? Years before, their healthy toddler son had suddenly died in an accident. How could they even consider the possibility of going through that wrenching heartache a second time? But as Mary and Jim prayed, they felt drawn to this tiny infant. They began to ask me to go places so they could volunteer to babysit for us. They agreed that they had felt God's grace sustain them through the loss of their dear son the first time, and He would be their Shepherd if He called them to enter the valley of the shadow of death a second time.

The adoption took place at Christmas time, much sooner than anyone imagined and before Luke was well. But God's promise, "I will go before you" (Isaiah 45:2), was comforting as the family stepped out in faith and received this little bundle with thanksgiving and rejoicing. Our friends decided to give him our name as his middle name and we were honored by that decision. And so after many treatments and much prayer, Luke did not die but became a healthy brother to three big sisters. He is a rascal at times, but he has a huge smile that has become a bright spot in all of our lives.

See now that I, myself am He! There is no god besides me.
I put to death and I bring to life, I have wounded and I
will heal, and no one can deliver out of my hand.
Deuteronomy 32:39

The Lord has done this, and it is marvelous in our eyes.
Psalm 118:23

Carolyn

It was spring break and I received a phone call, "Will you substitute for another foster family while they spend a week with their teenagers on a ski trip?" Our family loved to pitch in, and that's how Carolyn came to grace our family.

Carolyn had light pink skin, reddish blonde hair, and blue eyes. She looked like a sweet little Southern peach. I was delighted to show her off at a monthly neighborhood meeting. Carolyn slept peacefully in my arms, wrapped in a pink quilt with a lacy binding. One woman remarked that Carolyn was the loveliest baby she had ever seen.

Even several years later, this woman remembered that beautiful baby. I never had the heart to tell her the truth about Carolyn. This gorgeous baby would have been unwanted by many birth parents. She could have been destroyed by abortion before she ever took a breath, simply because an amniocentesis test would have shown that she had Down syndrome.

Carolyn had all the symptoms of retardation: the slanted eyes, the difficulty in drinking her bottle, the choking and sputtering. She would never be perfect by the world's standards. Throughout her life, she would struggle mentally, physically, and emotionally with the handicaps that come with Down syndrome. But does that mean she should not exist, that she doesn't belong on this earth? Of course not. She will teach many things about coming into God's kingdom as a little child that loves unconditionally and unreservedly. But she will also teach her adopted parents that God will supply all their needs, including an extra abundance of patience and perseverance when days get tough, and they will, no doubt. They will also experience the blessing of extending tender mercy to the helpless.

Did Carolyn become a wanted child? Yes, a family in Minnesota adopted her! They are providing a Christian home where she is learning that Jesus loves all the little children of the world. She now has a brother, sisters, and an extended family to watch her grow up and receive and give love.

The LORD is gracious and compassionate, slow to anger and rich in love. The LORD is good to all; he has compassion on all he has made.

Psalm 145:8, 9

CRIES FROM THE CRADLE

Sylvie

This beautiful, six-pound baby girl has the most gorgeous golden skin and brown curls that match her light brown eyes. Our college-aged daughter, who is an English major, picked the name Sylvie after a poet. But it reminds me of the dear woman from the Dominican Republic, Sylvia Head, who faithfully served in our church nursery for many years. She loved our children when they were babies and helped us with some other foster babies who have graced our home.

Sylvie came to our home right after Christmas. The weather was cold, and she almost seemed to disappear under a plaid blanket, she was so tiny. Her soft curls flattened out with the tiny cap she wore to keep the wind away. But her large eyes made my heart melt as she looked up with a sober stare.

Most babies are rather like lumps for a while but not Sylvie. She was strong and wiry; maybe she'll be a gymnast. We have prayed for each of the babies who have blessed our home with their presence, that their lives would serve the Lord Jesus and His kingdom. It has been fun to wonder about what talents and personality traits God has given them.

Sylvie suffered from colic, the dread syndrome of crying from stomachaches every night. I was so sleepy from walking her night after night that one time I actually put her diaper on backwards. The pediatrician said she gulps her bottle too fast and then suffered from a distended, tight stomach. She fought me when I took the bottle away and tipped her up to burp. She howled loudly and stiffened her tiny back as if to say, "No, I want it MY way." So for one of her bottles, I let her have her way. She eagerly guzzled the entire bottle, even though she struggled against air that slowed her sucking. She locked on to the nipple, triumphantly draining the bottle dry.

She was not a "spitter," though I still armed myself as usual with a cloth diaper. It was a good thing for nearly the entire contents of the bottle ended up in my lap! What an illustration this was that a stubborn determination to follow a course of action without taking heed to consequences could result in a lot of trouble.

My husband and I were both exhausted after some nights of only four hours sleep with this darling baby. Just when we wanted to go to bed, she began to cry inconsolably. Her sharp cries indicated that her pain was intense. We tried swaddling, pacifiers, changing nipples, changing formulas, medicine from the pediatrician, but nothing worked. My standard practice was to use the hymn, "What a Friend We Have in Jesus" as a lullaby for the babies. Most adoptive parents know this old standard, so the familiar tune in the baby's ear provides a way of making the transition a little smoother. But the double blessing has been that the words always minister to my broken heart as I hold each baby. I know that each one's time with us is brief, and they will not remember the love, the kisses, the first bath, the first smile that richly blessed our lives.

So one night as I held Sylvie close, the hymn's words floated through the darkened living room as I held the squalling blanketed bundle closely, and crooned softly in her tiny ear. But it was for my ears that the Holy Spirit brought the words from my memory to my lips. And it was for my pain that He died. "Oh, what needless pain we bear, All because we do not carry ev'rything to God in pray'r."

What a blessing this tiny bundle has been to our lives. God bless you, little Sylvie, and may you learn to follow His way.

> *"There is a way that seems right to a man,*
> *but in the end it leads to death."*
> Proverbs 14:12

> *"The Lord is a refuge for the oppressed, a stronghold in times of trouble. Those who know your name will trust in you, for you, Lord, have never forsaken those who seek you."*
> Psalm 9:9, 10

EMPTY ARMS

Tomas Has a New Name

Tomas has been a treasure wrapped in a brown paper bag. He was born with long, silky black hair, a beautiful olive complexion that went with his Hispanic heritage but also multiple problems that made people wince to look at his sweet face. Instead of an upper lip, a roof of his mouth, and a nose, he had a gaping hole and three odd balls of flesh attached to his incomplete nose. He couldn't suck, and he had only half a smile, so my first reaction was, *Lord, please have mercy on this pitiful child. Why did you make him like this?*

Tomas's parents didn't feel as if they could cope with the problems, so they asked the hospital to contact the welfare department. Someone called Bethany Christian Services. Since it was summer, many foster families were out of town, but the big-hearted Swanson family said, "We'll take him so he can learn about Jesus." What we didn't know is that God sent him to teach us about Jesus, too.

Tomas first stayed in our home when the Swansons were going out of town. Our son Eric likes to help with the foster babies, but this time he wasn't so sure he wanted to hold such an ugly baby. I must admit it took me about twenty-four hours to see past the deformities. We used a special, soft-squeeze bottle since he couldn't suck. The foster parent would place it in the hole where his mouth was half formed and squirt the formula into the back of his throat. It was odd.

A lady behind me in line at the checkout counter of the grocery store gasped, "You are sticking that bottle in the baby's nose."

"Yes," I said, "you're right. He has a cleft lip and a cleft palate."

Many times the next response I heard was in a disapproving tone, "Did the mother take drugs?" I generally replied, "We don't know why he was formed this way, but we have decided to care for him anyway."

But now that we have seen him lovingly held in his adoptive mother's arms and met the proud new daddy and thrilled big brother, we know the real reason. It was so the works of God might be revealed. The Lord provided a perfect family for this special baby! They had already adopted a baby twelve years ago who also was Hispanic and had a cleft palate. This boy was praying that God would send him a little brother. Not a sister but a brother! While this dear family was waiting for God to answer their prayers, they had been a host family to foreign children visiting in our country for surgical assistance. But then they went home to their own families. This special little guy would need surgery, too, but this time he was going to stay forever in his new home with his new name.

Open that crumpled, funny looking, brown paper bag, and what do you see inside? An amazing picture of redemption that has been acted out in our midst! Tomas was unlovely just as we are because of sin. He was helpless just as we are unable to save ourselves from the wrath of God. We have an elder Brother who is pleading for us to the Father, and Tomas now has a brother. At great cost, we were bought through Jesus' sacrifice of laying down His life on the cross, so one day we can go home to heaven forgiven and whole. There will be cost involved for this family; it will not be easy to parent this special-needs child, especially through the pain and heartache of multiple surgeries. But they are willing to die to self as they trust the Lord to give them wisdom and strength and as they keep sight of the joy to come when Tomas (soon to be Juan) is whole.

Jesus told us, "Whatever you did for one of the least of these brothers of mine, you did for me" (Matthew 25:40). We have been given a marvelous treasure hidden in the dark bag. We have seen Jesus through this tiny baby with a new name.

> *I will give you the treasures of darkness, riches stored in secret places, so that you may know that I am the* Lord, *the God of Israel, who summons you by name.*
> Isaiah 45:3

> *"Neither this man nor his parents sinned," said Jesus, "but this happened so that the work of God might be displayed in his life."*
> John 9:3

Mark

In another town, a mother chose not to parent her newborn. The nurse told her of an 800 number she could call to talk to a Christian adoption agency about making an adoption plan for the infant.

A staff member assured the confused woman that the next day when she was released from the hospital, the agency's social worker would receive the baby into her care. Before the social worker left for that long drive, she put us on alert, "Would you take a baby boy?"

As we celebrated the resurrection of the Savior on Easter, we welcomed a five-pound black baby boy. He was so tiny; his sleepers seemed to swallow him. It was our youngest daughter's turn to name the baby, and she called him Mark.

Mark grew quickly, but he was fussy. He cried day and night. But with three children to help hold and rock him, we managed. In early June the social worker offered to move him to another foster family. She knew I had my hands full, but she did not have a prospective family lined up yet. It would probably be a while before he was adopted.

Our family prayed and discussed the possible move. Even though it would be a welcome relief, we felt we should persevere with our heavenly assignment. So I told the social worker, "Our children have been earnestly praying for a family for little Mark, and we would miss seeing how God answers their prayers."

In June and July our son, Evan, was playing on a Dixie League baseball team for ten- and eleven-year-olds. As the season wrapped up, he had the honor of being invited to play on the all-stars team for a citywide tournament. We were thrilled to find that the coach of this special team was the beloved Mr. David Wilson, a black man who had an excellent reputation of being a caring, family man and whose own son was also on the all-stars. His patient, tireless enthusiasm brought out the best in his players, and he always used positive comments to train the boys towards good sportsmanship.

In God's design, this coach's eight-year-old daughter was drawn to our foster baby as we sat in the stands watching the baseball games. Because the players were from different teams, the parents and families did not know each other. As we gathered nightly while our team kept advancing through each round of the tournament, many assumed the black baby boy cuddled in Nikki's lap belonged to her family, not ours. Gradually, Nikki's mother and older sister became enchanted with this adorable baby with the lopsided grin.

It was a nail-biting, championship game. Our son, with perfect timing, hit a home run to tie the game. And to make it even more perfect, his grandparents (who love baseball) were visiting from out of town and could cheer Evan around the bases to home.

As we filed out of the stands that night, Grandma whispered in my ear, "I'm going to pray the Wilsons will adopt Mark."

My quick reply was "But, Mom, they have three children already."

She persisted, "They would be perfect, such a loving family."

The next week, Mrs. Wilson called on the phone.

"Could we babysit for you? We miss seeing Mark now that the tournament is over."

After several visits, the Wilsons contacted the adoption agency, Bethany Christian Services. They asked if another family was in line, or could they be considered for Mark's new family?

It was unusual for the agency to do, but they encouraged them to fill out the paperwork for the adoption.

Right after Labor Day, the Big Day came. Our prayers had been answered in a way that touched our hearts. Mark would become a member of the Wilson household! Our family cried as our sweet baby of four months moved to his new, forever family. But we rejoiced to know he would be close by where we could watch him grow up.

What we didn't realize was that a seed had been planted in our own hearts by watching the Wilsons' example. Maybe following their lead and making room for one more could fill the hole we felt. And to fast forward ten years, God not only blessed us with an adopted son the next year, but this son, Eric, and Mark became friends and ball players on the same team. Guess who their coach was? Mr. Wilson.

For whoever wants to save his life will lose it,
but whoever loses his life for me and for the gospel
will save it. What good is it for a man to gain
the whole world, yet forfeit his soul?
Mark 8: 35, 36

Rosemary

The winter sun slipped down behind the horizon. It had been a cold but sunny February day made special by the warmth of the celebration in our home.

My husband's mother, Granny B, as we affectionately call her, turned eighty years old. Our extended family members gathered from several cities to mark this memorable milestone. We dined on crab casserole and finished with a beautiful cake and a rousing "Happy Birthday" sung in four-part harmony.

Now the china and crystal were washed, and I was ready to put my feet up when the phone rang. The adoption agency asked, "Can you receive an infant into foster care?" It was unusual to pick up a baby late on a Sunday evening, but all the circumstances around this adorable, chubby girl turned out to be extraordinary.

The social worker told us that the birthmother had tried to parent the child for one month. She found the demands of parenting a newborn alone so overwhelming that she called the 800-number our agency provides for emergencies. She asked for care for her baby temporarily until she could decide if she should parent or release the baby for adoption. The policy in place was thirty days of free foster care and counseling, which included a workbook titled, *Baby and Me.*

The part of the equation that did not add up was the fact that the birthmother called a Christian agency, yet made it clear she was not a believer. In truth, she was not only uninterested but downright hostile towards Christianity. It was a puzzle to me how this sweet, dark-haired, dimpled beauty had arrived in our home.

I claimed the right to give this new darling her foster name because with her blue eyes and rosy, pink cheeks, she looked Irish, so the name Rosemary suited her perfectly. She was an easy baby; she liked to cuddle and coo. I dressed her in some of the smocked gowns that Granny B had sewn for our own daughters, and she looked adorable. Our whole family fell under Rosemary's spell. We felt God had graced our family in a special way by giving us the privilege of caring for this cutie pie. Amazingly, she began sleeping through the night shortly after she arrived. Now that was a major blessing.

The agency has certain regulations: after thirty days the birthmother has three choices: choose to parent; release the baby for adoption to a loving, well-screened, Christian couple; or begin paying for each additional day of foster care. During that month, the birth parents and even grandparents are welcome to visit the infant for a few hours at the agency's office.

After one week, we received a call came from our social worker: Rosemary's mother had changed her mind. She decided she wanted her baby back the next day. I packed up her things and put the shopping bag by the door. The next morning, the social worker called again. I was not to bring Rosemary but to unpack the shopping bag and keep her. The voice at the other end sighed and admitted this was the most difficult client she had ever worked with in many years of counseling. As she elaborated on the situation, the mystery of how the birthmother called us was solved for me. The girl was a rebellious teenager who had run away from a Christian home. She was angry and wanted no part of her parents' religion, but she had parents who loved her and her baby. Now my husband and I understood. Rosemary had grandparents who were covering her in prayer.

Just as this girl felt she didn't need God or her parents' help, I had come to the same conclusion in my spiritual walk with the Lord. I had built up barriers to my heavenly Father's help and trusted in my own strength. I had allowed pride to fill my heart. We had been foster parents to many babies, so I felt self-sufficient in drawing curtains over my emotions. Yes, I could handle this, and I looked down on others who were not willing to risk a broken heart for service in God's kingdom. In Bible terms, I had become a Pharisee with a holier-than-thou attitude. My lack of humility made it impossible for me to ask for my Father's help, so I continued to care for this baby in my own strength.

Three weeks went by quickly. Through our church, we were hosting an interesting doctor and his wife, who were speakers in a special renewal weekend of testimonies. They shared in holding little Rosemary and enjoyed her endearing smiles.

Then another call came. The thirty days were up, and the birthmother had decided to parent. I was to pack up the baby's things. I dissolved to tears. How could I turn her over to a young mother who was troubled and lacked family support? This was painful for all of us.

I swallowed my pride and admitted how devastating it was to surrender this sweet baby to a doubtful future. God in His mercy had provided me with *in-house* prayer support from this visiting couple. Together, we committed this tiny girl into His hands.

Once again, I filled the shopping bag with diapers, bottles, formula, and a few baby clothes and had it sitting by the front door. I changed Rosemary's diaper one last time, when the phone rang. The birthmother had changed her mind again and signed the release form. We were asked to keep the baby another week until the adoption could be set in motion. That meant a pre-adoption physical, done by a Christian pediatrician who volunteers his time.

Finally, a waiting couple received a call, giving them the news for which they had been waiting patiently a long time. "We have a two-month-old baby girl for you—your new daughter!"

In the morning O Lord, you hear my voice; in the morning I lay my requests before you and wait in expectation.
Psalm 5:3

Epilogue

Recently, I was walking at the Commons, a park near our home, when a handsome young black man approached me with his arms wide open! He enveloped me in a huge hug! It took a few moments to recognize him. Our families had been friends long before his Christmas adoption through Bethany, when he moved from our family into their home. Henry and I have had the privilege of watching him grow up and flourish in a Christian home. He was one of the babies whose story is told in The Cries from the Cradle section of our book.

It has been 15 years since Empty Arms was released and Ann and I have been amazed at God's plan. It was greater than we could have ever imagined! The message of forgiveness, hope and healing has reached a far larger audience and now we pray Empty Arms will impact and reach the next generation. Visitors have come to The Wall not only from all over the United States but also from Kenya, Belarus, Canada and Norway! The Memorial is a sacred space that proclaims the message that we can have assurance of the hope of heaven.

"We have this hope as an anchor for the soul, firm and secure. It enters the inner sanctuary behind the curtain, where Jesus, who went before us, has entered on our behalf..."
Hebrews 6:19-20a

What comfort can be found in the arms of our Shepherd!

Wendy J. Williams

BIOGRAPHIES

Ann M. Caldwell lives on Lookout Mountain, Tennessee, with her husband Mark and three children, Mac, Kay, and Ben. She attends Lookout Mountain Presbyterian Church, where she is active in Women in the Church and teaches Sunday school. She and her husband have been involved in the National Memorial for the Unborn since its inception, and she placed her plaque on the day The Memorial was dedicated. She served on the board of The Memorial and is also active in PTA.

Wendy J. Williams lives on Lookout Mountain, Tennessee, with her physician husband Henry. They have four children and have been foster parents for the past twenty years. They have fostered over twenty newborn babies awaiting adoption and have provided shelter to women in crisis pregnancies. Wendy served on the board of the National Memorial for the Unborn. She is the author of *Scripture Pictures*, a pocket-sized book that has sold over two million copies. She has traveled to Poland, Russia, and Cuba on mission trips, and she and her husband lived on a Navajo Indian reservation for two years, leading Bible studies for children and adults. They have also been active in a Christian medical relief program called Chernobyl Children. Through many of life's troubles she has found Jesus to be faithful.

INDEX

Contributors of Stories Behind the Plaques	Plaque Location on The Wall	Page Number in Book
1. Averie Alverson	5-I-22	39
2. Stacy B.	5-F-7	119
3. Ann Caldwell	4-N-28	136
4. Mary Louise Cann	2-C-14	157
5. Linda Cochrane	4-N-12	49
6. Mary Cowan	3-J-9	88
7. Julie Crockett	9-F-6	60
8. Brenda Darnell	7-I-25	47
9. Rosalie DiMaggio	4-O-15	44
10. Sharon Dishaw	1-H-4,5	154
11. Laurie Duffield	9-K-13	37
12. Carol Everett	5-O-14	51
13. Christine Fischer	......	118
14. Debbie Garriock	4-I-22	72
15. Shelley Goodell	......	128
16. Cynthia Hardeman	8-C-9	35
17. Carrie Harless	8-F-29	19
18. William Heim	8-F-9	106
19. Crystal Shannon Henderson	2-O-15	21
20. Cindy Hendrickson	10-F-6	112
21. Sue Burton Illig	6-B-13	95
22. Lance Irwin	5-G-1	125
23. Debbie Johnson	6-N-19	75
24. Karen K.	7-C-16	93
25. Carolyn Kasdorf	5-M-10, 5-N-10	98
26. Wanda King	6-E-16	158
27. Holly Lewis	7-H-9	162
28. Candy Little	6-A-12	57
29. Jolinda Lynch	8-E-18	149

30.	Patti M.	8-G-13	30
31.	Sherri Madill	6-I-22	53
32.	Sydna Masse	9-L-15	55
33.	Teressa	8-L-23	164
34.	Scott Miller	5-J-10	69
35.	Marlena Moore	9-M-21	65
36.	Debbie Niehaus	6-K-21	33
37.	Denise Perehinec	3-F-23	123
38.	Joan Phillips	2-D-17	83
39.	Athlynn Reeves	1-K-9	166
40.	Kathleen Reynolds	2-K-29	91
41.	Sue Ann Schumacher	7-B-4	28
42.	Pam Shaffer	5-G-10	121
43.	Mary E. Stanley	4-O-19	115
44.	Elsa Stewart	2-G-13	86
45.	Patty Stewart	5-K-26	77
46.	Anne Swafford	4-O-28	133
47.	Dee Dee Swilling	6-H-24	67
48.	Donna T.	7-K-18	147
49.	Linda Keener Thomas	2-K-13	143
50.	William Zazeckie	3-N-5, 3-N-6	109

Anonymous Contributions

Names on the Plaques	Plaque Location on The Wall	Page Number in Book
51. AMY—MY LOVE	2-K-18	160
52. BABY	……	24
53. BABY	……	103
54. BABY ANGEL LUTHER	10-C-23	27
55. DANIEL	2-F-9	139
56. JEREMIAH PAUL	6-B-8	152
57. OUR PRECIOUS JESSI	4-A-17	79
58. WILLIAM ANTHONY	10-A-10, 11	101

Contributors of Poems

Heidi Hetsteck
Mareta Keener Thomas
Carolyn Rice
Jeanne Vadala

After auction at U.S. Bankruptcy Court

Rooms demolished where abortions took place

Granite wall installed

National Memorial for the Unborn opens

Made in the USA
Columbia, SC
07 June 2025

59056930R00137